Leaner Startup with GenAI

AI-enhanced entrepreneurship journey

By Arup Maity

Leaner Startup With GenAI

AI-enhanced entrepreneurship journey

By Arup Maity

© Arup Maity

Other than all my teachers, mentors, friends, co-workers and of course family, the one I need to thank most for this book are the several GenAI models that I utilized for researching and writing this book to the fullest extent possible

Prologue:

The first light of dawn breaks over Metro Manila as I reflect on the whirlwind week behind me. Our team at Xamun has just wrapped up a major release, pushing the boundaries of what's possible in AI-powered software development. I'm Arup Maity, and my journey to this moment has been anything but ordinary. For over two decades, I've navigated the intersections of construction, real estate, and software engineering. This unique perspective, bridging traditional industries and cutting-edge technology, has shaped my vision for the future of entrepreneurship – a future I'm thrilled to share with you in this book.

But make no mistake: while my experiences form the backbone of this narrative, this book is really about you. It's for the dreamers, the innovators, and the risk-takers who are bold enough to shape tomorrow. We're entering a new era of entrepreneurship, one where industry boundaries blur and the potential for impact is boundless.

In the pages that follow, we'll explore together how the fusion of lean startup principles and generative AI is reshaping the landscape of innovation across sectors. I'll share with you practical strategies, cutting-edge tools, and real-world case studies that I've encountered and developed throughout my career – strategies that will equip you to thrive in this new paradigm.

I'll draw from my experiences leading software product engineering at BlastAsia, developing AI-powered platforms like Xamun that accelerate software development 4x faster, and creating Steer to revolutionize construction project monitoring. Through concepts and case studies, we'll uncover how AI can turbocharge the lean startup methodology in ways I never thought possible when I started my career.

We'll explore how AI models can generate and test hypotheses at lightning speed, create and iterate on prototypes in real-time, and analyze vast swathes of market data in the blink of an eye. Whether you're in software development, construction, or any other industry ripe for disruption, I'll show you how to leverage AI to build leaner, more efficient startups.

Whether you're a first-time founder with a world-changing idea, a seasoned entrepreneur looking to stay ahead of the curve, or an innovator within an established organization, I wrote this book to be your guide to navigating the exciting frontier of AI-enhanced entrepreneurship.

Throughout this book, you'll encounter references to various AI and GenAI tools that can assist at different stages of the startup lifecycle. However, it's crucial to note that these mentions are not endorsements. The AI landscape is rapidly evolving, and new tools emerge while others may become obsolete. I encourage you to use these references as a starting point to explore and find the best-suited tools available at the time you're reading this. Always conduct your own research, consider your specific needs, and stay updated on the latest developments in AI tools and platforms.

Now, I'll be honest – some of these ideas might seem a bit out there. You might be thinking, "Can't I just use Excel?" Sure you can! This book isn't a step-by-step guide. It's about expanding your mind to what's possible. I want to spark ideas about automating the tedious (but crucial) parts of your journey, helping you succeed faster and easier.

So, welcome to the world of Leaner Startup with GenAI. Together, we'll bridge the gap between traditional industries and cutting-edge AI, between academic theory and practical application, between local insights and global opportunities. The future of innovation starts here, and I promise you, it's leaner, faster, and more exciting than anything I've seen in my 20+ years in this field.

Are you ready to embark on this journey with me? Let's build the future – leaner, smarter, and powered by AI.

Table of Content:

Prologue: 4
Table of Content: 6
Chapter 1: The Dawn of a New Entrepreneurial Era 8
Chapter 2: Fundamentals of Lean Startup 14
Chapter 3: Understanding Generative AI 22
Chapter 4: The Convergence: Lean Startup meets GenAI 29
Chapter 5: AI-Enhanced Lean Canvas and Business Model Generation 36
Chapter 6: Rapid Prototyping and MVP Development with AI 44
Chapter 7: Optimizing the Build-Measure-Learn Cycle with AI ... 52
Chapter 8: AI-Powered Customer Discovery and Validation 59
Chapter 9: AI-Driven Growth Hacking and Marketing Strategies 66
Chapter 10: Lean Analytics with AI 74
Chapter 11: AI for Agile Financial Management in Startups 81
Chapter 12: AI-Assisted Pitch Deck and Investor Relations 88
Chapter 13: AI for Lean Team Management and Collaboration 96
Chapter 14: Scaling with AI: From Startup to Enterprise 103
Chapter 15: Ethical Considerations and Challenges in AI-Driven Lean Startups 111
Chapter 16: Future Trends: The Leaner Startup Ecosystem 118
Chapter 17: Building the Future with Leaner Startups and GenAI .. 126
About the Author 148

"If I have seen further than others, it is by standing upon the shoulders of giants."
- Sir Isaac Newton

Chapter 1: The Dawn of a New Entrepreneurial Era

Introduction

In the ever-evolving world of entrepreneurship, we stand at the cusp of a revolutionary transformation. The convergence of time-tested business principles, lean methodologies, and cutting-edge artificial intelligence is reshaping how we conceive, build, and scale startups. This chapter explores the journey from the tumultuous days of the Dotcom era to the emergence of the Lean Startup methodology, and now, to the exciting frontier of AI-enhanced entrepreneurship. As we embark on this exploration, we'll uncover how these shifts are not just changing the tools at our disposal, but fundamentally altering the very nature of innovation and business creation.

The Evolution of the Startup Landscape

From Dotcom Boom to Bust: Lessons in Humility

The late 1990s marked a period of unprecedented excitement and investment in the tech industry. The rapid growth of the internet sparked a gold rush mentality, with investors pouring billions into unproven business models.

Case Study: Pets.com

Pets.com, launched in August 1998, became an iconic symbol of the Dotcom bubble. Despite raising $82.5 million in an IPO in February 2000, the company collapsed just nine months later.

Key Factors in Failure:

1. Unsustainable business model: High costs of shipping heavy pet products eroded margins.
2. Premature scaling: Massive advertising spend before proving the market.
3. Lack of customer understanding: Overestimated online pet supply demand.

Lesson Learned: The Pets.com story highlighted the dangers of prioritizing growth over sustainable business practices and the importance of validating market assumptions before scaling.

The Birth of Lean: Steve Blank and Customer Development

In the aftermath of the Dotcom crash, entrepreneurs and investors sought new approaches to building startups. Steve Blank, a serial entrepreneur and academic, introduced the concept of Customer Development in his 2005 book "The Four Steps to the Epiphany."

Case Study: IMVU

IMVU, a social entertainment company co-founded by Eric Ries, became an early adopter and proving ground for Blank's customer development methodology.

Key Strategies Employed:

1. Continuous customer feedback loops
2. Rapid iteration based on user behavior
3. Focus on metrics that matter for growth

Results: By 2010, IMVU had 40 million registered users and was generating $40 million in revenue.

Lesson Learned: The success of IMVU demonstrated the power of customer-centric development and data-driven decision making in building a sustainable startup.

The Lean Startup Revolution: Eric Ries Codifies the Method

Building on Blank's work and his experiences at IMVU, Eric Ries published "The Lean Startup" in 2011, popularizing a methodology that emphasized experimentation, iterative product releases, and validated learning.

Key Principles of the Lean Startup:

1. Build-Measure-Learn feedback loop
2. Minimum Viable Product (MVP)
3. Pivot or Persevere decisions
4. Innovation accounting

Case Study: Dropbox

Dropbox, founded in 2007, exemplifies the successful application of Lean Startup principles.

Lean Strategies Used:

1. MVP: Initial product demo video to gauge interest
2. Continuous iteration based on user feedback
3. Growth hacking techniques for user acquisition

Results: Dropbox grew from 100,000 registered users in September 2008 to 4 million by January 2010. By 2018, it had over 500 million registered users.

Lesson Learned: Dropbox's journey illustrates how lean principles can guide a startup from initial concept to large-scale success, emphasizing the power of MVPs and data-driven growth strategies.

Introduction to Generative AI (GenAI) and its Potential Impact

As we enter the 2020s, a new technological revolution is underway: the rise of Generative AI (GenAI). This subset of artificial intelligence is capable of creating new content, from text and images to code and product designs.

Key Capabilities of GenAI:

1. Natural language processing and generation
2. Image and video creation
3. Code generation and completion
4. Data analysis and pattern recognition

Potential Impacts on Startups:

1. Accelerated product development cycles
2. Enhanced customer understanding through data analysis
3. Automated content creation for marketing and engagement
4. Improved decision-making through predictive analytics

Case Study: GitHub Copilot

GitHub Copilot, launched in 2021, is an AI pair programmer that can generate code snippets based on natural language descriptions.

Early Results:

1. 40% of newly written code in supported languages is suggested by Copilot
2. Developers report increased productivity and faster problem-solving

Potential Impact: Tools like GitHub Copilot could dramatically accelerate the MVP development process, allowing startups to iterate and validate ideas faster than ever before.

Conclusion

The startup landscape has undergone a dramatic transformation since the heady days of the Dotcom era. From the hard-learned lessons of the bubble's burst emerged the customer-centric, data-driven approaches of Customer Development and the Lean Startup methodology. These frameworks have reshaped how entrepreneurs approach building and scaling businesses, emphasizing validation, iteration, and sustainable growth over mere hype and rapid expansion.

Now, as we stand on the brink of the GenAI revolution, we are poised for another leap forward. The integration of Generative AI into the lean startup process promises to accelerate innovation, enhance decision-making, and open up new possibilities for creative problem-solving. However, as history has taught us, technology alone is not a panacea. The successful startups of tomorrow will be those that can harness the power of AI while staying true to the core principles of customer focus, validated learning, and adaptability that have become the hallmarks of successful entrepreneurship.

Key Takeaways:

1. The Dotcom crash highlighted the importance of sustainable business models and market validation.
2. Customer Development and Lean Startup methodologies emerged as responses to the failures of the Dotcom era, emphasizing customer-centric, data-driven approaches.
3. Successful application of lean principles, as seen in companies like IMVU and Dropbox, can lead to sustainable growth and market success.
4. Generative AI represents the next frontier in startup evolution, offering tools to accelerate development, enhance customer understanding, and improve decision-making.
5. The integration of GenAI with lean methodologies has the potential to revolutionize how startups are built and scaled, but must be approached with the same rigor and customer focus that defines the lean approach.

As we move forward, the challenge and opportunity for entrepreneurs lie in effectively combining the wisdom gained from past failures and successes with the immense potential of new AI technologies. The future of startups is not just lean, but intelligently augmented, opening up new horizons for innovation and growth.

"On Day One, a start-up is a faith-based initiative built on guesses."
- Steve Blank

Chapter 2: Fundamentals of Lean Startup

Introduction

In Chapter 1, we traced the evolution of the startup landscape from the tumultuous days of the Dotcom era to the emergence of more disciplined, customer-centric approaches to entrepreneurship. We saw how the failures of the early 2000s led to the development of Steve Blank's Customer Development process and eventually to Eric Ries's Lean Startup methodology. Now, as we stand on the cusp of the Generative AI revolution, it's crucial to have a solid understanding of these foundational concepts that have reshaped the way we build and scale startups.

The Lean Startup methodology, born out of the need for a more efficient and less risky approach to startup creation, has become a cornerstone of modern entrepreneurship. It provides a framework that allows entrepreneurs to navigate the uncertain waters of innovation with greater confidence and efficiency. As we prepare to explore how Generative AI can enhance and accelerate these processes, we must first grasp the core principles that underpin the Lean Startup approach.

In this chapter, we'll delve deep into the fundamental concepts of the Lean Startup method. We'll explore the key principles that guide lean thinking, unpack the Build-Measure-Learn feedback loop that drives continuous improvement, and examine the concept of the Minimum Viable Product (MVP) that allows for rapid validation of business ideas.

Through real-world case studies, we'll see how these principles have been applied successfully by startups across various industries, demonstrating the versatility and power of the Lean Startup method. From Zappos's innovative approach to validating the online shoe market to Airbnb's evolution through careful application of the Build-Measure-Learn loop, these examples will illustrate how lean principles can be put into practice.

As we explore these concepts, keep in mind the potential impact of Generative AI that we touched upon in Chapter 1. The fundamental principles of the Lean Startup method remain as relevant as ever in the AI era, but as we'll see in later chapters, AI tools have the potential to supercharge these processes, allowing for even faster iteration, more sophisticated data analysis, and new forms of product creation.

By the end of this chapter, you'll have a solid grasp of the Lean Startup fundamentals, preparing you for our exploration of how these principles can be enhanced and accelerated through the application of Generative AI. Let's begin our deep dive into the world of Lean Startup methodology.

1. Key Principles of the Lean Startup Method

The Lean Startup method, popularized by Eric Ries, is built on several fundamental principles that guide entrepreneurs in their journey from idea to successful business. Let's explore these key principles:

a) Validated Learning

At the core of the Lean Startup method is the concept of validated learning. This principle emphasizes the importance of rapidly testing your assumptions about your business model and product through real-world experiments.

b) Innovation Accounting

This principle involves using actionable metrics to measure progress, set up milestones, and prioritize work. It's about measuring what matters for your specific business model.

c) Small Batches

The idea is to work in small batches or increments, allowing for quicker turnaround and faster learning cycles.

d) Continuous Deployment

For software startups, this means putting out new versions of the product as often as possible to gather user feedback quickly.

e) Five Whys

This is a problem-solving technique used to get to the root cause of problems by asking "why" five times.

Case Study: Zappos

Zappos, the online shoe retailer, exemplifies the application of Lean Startup principles, particularly validated learning and innovation accounting.

Key Actions:

1. Initially, founder Nick Swinmurn photographed shoes from local stores and posted them online to test demand.
2. Used actionable metrics to measure not just sales, but customer satisfaction and repeat purchases.

Results:

- By 2009, Zappos reached $1 billion in annual gross merchandise sales.
- In the same year, Amazon acquired Zappos for $1.2 billion.

Lesson Learned: Zappos' success demonstrates how validated learning can help prove a business model before significant investment, and how focusing on the right metrics can drive sustainable growth.

2. Build-Measure-Learn Feedback Loop

The Build-Measure-Learn feedback loop is the central mechanism of the Lean Startup methodology. It's a cyclical process designed to turn ideas into products, measure customer response, and then decide whether to pivot or persevere.

Build

In this phase, the focus is on building a Minimum Viable Product (MVP) that allows you to start the learning process as quickly as possible.

Measure

This involves deciding what metrics are important and using innovation accounting to analyze the results of your experiments.

Learn

Based on the data gathered, entrepreneurs must decide whether to pivot (make a fundamental change to the product or strategy) or persevere (continue on the current path with refinements).

Case Study: Airbnb

Airbnb's journey is a perfect illustration of the Build-Measure-Learn feedback loop in action.

Key Actions:

1. Build: Started with a simple website offering air mattresses in the founders' apartment during a design conference.
2. Measure: Tracked bookings and user feedback.
3. Learn: Realized people were interested in unique spaces, not just cheap accommodations.

Results:

- Pivoted from air mattresses to a wide variety of unique accommodations.
- As of 2021, Airbnb has over 4 million hosts worldwide.

Lesson Learned: Airbnb's success shows how the Build-Measure-Learn loop can help a company evolve its product based on real user feedback and behavior.

3. Minimum Viable Product (MVP) Concept

The Minimum Viable Product is a core concept in the Lean Startup methodology. It's the version of a new product that allows a team to collect the maximum amount of validated learning about customers with the least effort.

Characteristics of an MVP:

1. Has enough value that people are willing to use it or buy it initially
2. Demonstrates enough future benefit to retain early adopters
3. Provides a feedback loop to guide future development

Types of MVPs:

1. Concierge MVP: Manually provided service to a small number of users
2. Wizard of Oz MVP: Appears to be a functional product, but operations are manual behind the scenes
3. Landing Page MVP: A web page describing the product to gauge interest
4. Piecemeal MVP: Uses existing tools to deliver the product

Case Study: Buffer

Buffer, a social media management platform, used a series of MVPs to validate their business idea and grow their user base.

Key Actions:

1. Started with a simple landing page MVP describing the product and gauging interest.
2. Built a minimal product that only allowed scheduling tweets.
3. Continuously added features based on user feedback.

Results:

- Within 9 months of launch, Buffer had 100,000 users.
- As of 2021, Buffer has over 75,000 paying customers.

Lesson Learned: Buffer's approach shows how starting with a simple MVP and iterating based on user feedback can lead to product-market fit and sustainable growth.

Conclusion

The Lean Startup methodology provides a framework for entrepreneurs to efficiently create and manage startups, fostering innovation in an environment of extreme uncertainty. By focusing on validated learning through the Build-Measure-Learn feedback loop and the use of Minimum Viable Products, startups can reduce the risk of failure and increase their chances of building something customers actually want.

The case studies of Zappos, Airbnb, and Buffer demonstrate that these principles are not just theoretical concepts, but practical tools that can be applied across various industries and business models. They show how starting small, measuring the right things, and being willing to pivot based on customer feedback can lead to remarkable success.

As we move forward into an era where Generative AI is becoming increasingly prevalent, these fundamental principles of the Lean Startup method remain crucial. In fact, they may become even more important as AI tools allow for faster iteration and more complex data analysis. The challenge for entrepreneurs will be to leverage these new technologies while staying true to the customer-centric, data-driven approach that defines the Lean Startup methodology.

Key Takeaways:

1. The Lean Startup method is built on principles of validated learning, innovation accounting, and rapid iteration.
2. The Build-Measure-Learn feedback loop is the core mechanism for turning ideas into successful products through continuous improvement.

3. The Minimum Viable Product (MVP) concept allows startups to start the learning process quickly with minimal resources.
4. Successful companies like Zappos, Airbnb, and Buffer have demonstrated the effectiveness of Lean Startup principles in real-world scenarios.
5. These fundamental principles remain relevant and can be enhanced as we enter the era of Generative AI in entrepreneurship.

By mastering these fundamentals, entrepreneurs can build a strong foundation for leveraging advanced technologies and methodologies in their startup journey.

"Aristotle founded or discovered logic by observing the world. ChatGPT thinks logically. Why? Because it notices all the logic in the data in its training set" - **Stephen Wolfram**

Chapter 3: Understanding Generative AI

Introduction

In the previous chapters, we explored the evolution of startup methodologies from the Dotcom era to the Lean Startup approach. We delved into the fundamental principles that have reshaped how entrepreneurs build and scale their businesses. Now, as we stand on the brink of another technological revolution, it's time to turn our attention to a powerful new tool that has the potential to supercharge these lean methodologies: Generative AI (GenAI).

Generative AI represents a paradigm shift in how we interact with and leverage artificial intelligence. Unlike traditional AI systems that are designed to analyze and interpret existing data, GenAI has the remarkable ability to create new, original content. This capability has profound implications for startups and established businesses alike, offering unprecedented opportunities for innovation, efficiency, and creativity.

In this chapter, we'll demystify Generative AI, exploring its core concepts, the various types of GenAI systems, and their current capabilities and limitations. By understanding these fundamentals, we'll lay the groundwork for later chapters where we'll examine how GenAI can be integrated with Lean Startup principles to create even more powerful and efficient approaches to building successful businesses.

1. What is GenAI?

Generative AI refers to artificial intelligence systems that can create new content, rather than simply analyzing or categorizing existing data. These systems use machine learning algorithms, typically deep learning neural networks, to identify patterns in vast amounts of training data and then use these patterns to generate new, original outputs.

Key Characteristics of GenAI:

1. Creativity: Ability to produce novel content
2. Autonomy: Can generate output with minimal human input
3. Versatility: Applicable across various domains (text, image, audio, etc.)
4. Continuous Learning: Can improve performance over time with more data

Case Study: OpenAI's GPT-3

OpenAI's GPT-3 (Generative Pre-trained Transformer 3) is one of the most prominent examples of GenAI in action.

Key Features:

1. 175 billion parameters, making it one of the largest language models
2. Trained on a diverse range of internet text
3. Capable of generating human-like text across various styles and topics

Real-world Application: The Guardian, a British newspaper, used GPT-3 to write an entire article in 2020.

Results:

- The AI wrote eight different versions of the article
- Humans edited and compiled these versions into a final piece
- The article was coherent and raised thoughtful points about AI's potential and risks

Lesson Learned: GPT-3 demonstrated that GenAI can produce high-quality, creative content that rivals human-generated work, while also highlighting the ongoing need for human oversight and editing.

2. Types of GenAI

Generative AI encompasses a wide range of applications across various domains. Here are some of the main types:

a) Text Generation

Systems that can produce written content, from short phrases to long-form articles.

b) Image Generation

AI that can create, edit, or manipulate visual content.

c) Code Generation

AI capable of writing or completing code snippets and even entire programs.

d) Audio Generation

Systems that can create music, speech, or other audio content.

e) Video Generation

AI that can produce or manipulate video content.

Case Study: DALL-E 2 by OpenAI

DALL-E 2 is a prime example of image generation GenAI.

Key Features:

1. Creates images from text descriptions
2. Can edit existing images
3. Understands complex concepts and relationships

Real-world Application: Cosmopolitan magazine used DALL-E 2 to create the world's first AI-generated magazine cover in 2022.

Results:

- The cover was created based on the prompt: "wide-angle shot from below of a female astronaut with an athletic feminine body walking with swagger toward camera on Mars in an infinite universe, synthwave digital art"
- The final image was chosen from over 100 AI-generated options

Lesson Learned: DALL-E 2 showcased how GenAI can revolutionize creative processes, enabling rapid prototyping and exploration of visual ideas while also raising questions about the future of human artists and designers.

3. Current Capabilities and Limitations

As powerful as GenAI systems are, it's crucial to understand both their capabilities and limitations.

Current Capabilities:

1. **Natural Language Processing**: Advanced language understanding and generation.
2. **Multimodal Learning**: Ability to work across different types of data (text, image, audio).
3. **Transfer Learning**: Applying knowledge from one domain to another.
4. **Few-Shot Learning**: Ability to learn from a small number of examples.

Limitations:

1. **Lack of True Understanding**: GenAI doesn't truly comprehend the content it generates.
2. **Biases in Output**: Can reflect and amplify biases present in training data.
3. **Hallucination**: May generate plausible-sounding but incorrect information.
4. **Resource Intensity**: Requires significant computational power and data.

Case Study: GitHub Copilot

GitHub Copilot, developed by GitHub and OpenAI, is a code generation AI tool.

Key Features:

1. Suggests code completions in real-time
2. Works across multiple programming languages
3. Learns from the context of the current file and related files

Real-world Application: A study conducted by GitHub in 2022 examined the impact of Copilot on developer productivity.

Results:

- Developers completed tasks 55% faster with Copilot
- 60-75% of users reported feeling more fulfilled with their work when using Copilot
- However, 40% of the code suggestions contained security vulnerabilities when tested

Lesson Learned: GitHub Copilot demonstrated the potential of GenAI to significantly boost productivity in software development. However, it also highlighted the need for human oversight, especially in areas like security, where AI may not fully understand the implications of its suggestions.

Conclusion

Generative AI represents a quantum leap in artificial intelligence capabilities, offering tools that can create, innovate, and problem-solve in ways that were once the exclusive domain of human creativity. From GPT-3's ability to generate human-like text to DALL-E 2's capacity for creating visual art, and GitHub Copilot's code generation prowess, GenAI is already making significant impacts across various industries.

As we've seen, these tools offer immense potential for enhancing productivity, sparking creativity, and opening up new avenues for innovation. However, they also come with limitations and challenges that must be carefully considered and managed.

For entrepreneurs and startups, understanding GenAI is no longer optional – it's becoming a crucial component of staying competitive in a rapidly evolving technological landscape. As we move forward in this book, we'll explore how these powerful AI capabilities can be integrated with Lean Startup methodologies to create more efficient, innovative, and successful businesses.

The key will be to leverage the strengths of GenAI while being mindful of its limitations, always keeping the core principles of customer-centricity and validated learning at the forefront of our approach. By doing so, we can harness the full potential of this technology to build the next generation of groundbreaking startups.

Key Takeaways:

1. Generative AI is a type of artificial intelligence capable of creating original content across various domains (text, image, code, audio, video).
2. Major types of GenAI include text generation (like GPT-3), image generation (like DALL-E 2), and code generation (like GitHub Copilot).
3. GenAI offers significant capabilities in natural language processing, multimodal learning, transfer learning, and few-shot learning.
4. Current limitations include lack of true understanding, potential for biases, tendency to "hallucinate" incorrect information, and high resource requirements.
5. While GenAI can dramatically enhance productivity and creativity, it requires human oversight to ensure quality, relevance, and safety of outputs.
6. For startups, understanding and leveraging GenAI is becoming crucial for innovation and competitiveness in the modern business landscape.

As we move forward, we'll explore how these powerful AI tools can be integrated with Lean Startup principles to create even more efficient and innovative approaches to building successful businesses.

"The future is already here - it's just not evenly distributed."
- William Gibson

Chapter 4: The Convergence: Lean Startup meets GenAI

Introduction

In the previous chapters, we've explored the evolution of startup methodologies, delved into the core principles of the Lean Startup approach, and unveiled the transformative potential of Generative AI. Now, we stand at an exciting intersection where these two powerful concepts converge. This convergence promises to revolutionize the way we build, measure, and learn in the startup ecosystem.

The Lean Startup methodology, with its emphasis on rapid iteration, customer feedback, and data-driven decision making, has already transformed how entrepreneurs approach building businesses. Generative AI, with its ability to create, innovate, and process vast amounts of data, is poised to take these lean principles to new heights. In this chapter, we'll explore how GenAI can enhance and accelerate the Lean Startup process, potentially reshaping the landscape of entrepreneurship and innovation.

We'll examine how GenAI can be applied to each stage of the Lean Startup cycle, from ideation to validation to scaling. Through case studies and practical examples, we'll illustrate how this powerful technology is already being used to supercharge startup growth and efficiency. Let's dive into this exciting new frontier where lean methodology meets cutting-edge AI.

How GenAI Enhances the Lean Startup Process

Generative AI has the potential to enhance each core principle of the Lean Startup methodology. Let's explore how:

1. Validated Learning

GenAI can accelerate the process of forming and testing hypotheses by:

- Generating multiple business hypotheses based on market data
- Simulating customer behaviors and market conditions
- Analyzing vast amounts of customer feedback data quickly

2. Innovation Accounting

GenAI can improve how startups measure and communicate progress by:

- Automatically generating and analyzing key performance indicators (KPIs)

- Providing predictive analytics for future growth trajectories
- Creating detailed, data-driven reports for stakeholders

3. Minimum Viable Product (MVP)

GenAI can revolutionize the creation and iteration of MVPs by:

- Rapidly generating product prototypes based on specifications
- Creating multiple variations of product designs for A/B testing
- Automating parts of the development process, such as code generation

Case Study: Airbnb's Pricing Algorithm

While not strictly a GenAI application, Airbnb's use of machine learning for dynamic pricing illustrates how AI can enhance core Lean Startup principles.

Key Features:

1. Uses machine learning to analyze over 70 factors influencing pricing
2. Provides hosts with pricing suggestions to maximize bookings and revenue
3. Continuously learns and adapts based on booking data

Results:

- Hosts using the tool saw a 5% increase in booking probability
- Over 60% of Airbnb listings use the suggested prices

Lesson Learned: This case demonstrates how AI can enhance validated learning by continuously testing and refining pricing hypotheses, and improve innovation accounting by directly impacting key metrics like booking rates and revenue.

Accelerating the Build-Measure-Learn Cycle with AI

The Build-Measure-Learn cycle is at the heart of the Lean Startup methodology. GenAI has the potential to dramatically accelerate each phase of this cycle:

1. Build

GenAI can speed up the building process by:

- Generating code for software products
- Creating design mockups and prototypes
- Automating content creation for marketing materials

2. Measure

GenAI can enhance measurement by:

- Processing and analyzing large volumes of user data in real-time
- Identifying patterns and trends that humans might miss
- Generating comprehensive reports and visualizations of key metrics

3. Learn

GenAI can accelerate learning by:

- Quickly synthesizing insights from diverse data sources
- Generating hypotheses for future iterations
- Providing predictive analytics to guide decision-making

Case Study: Stitch Fix's Hybrid Design Process

Stitch Fix, an online personal styling service, uses a combination of human creativity and AI to design new clothing items.

Key Features:

1. AI analyzes customer feedback, purchase history, and fashion trends
2. The system generates new design elements based on this data
3. Human designers curate and refine the AI-generated ideas

Results:

- In 2017, Stitch Fix launched its first AI-designed products
- By 2021, the company had created over 30 new brands using this hybrid approach
- This process has significantly reduced the time from concept to market-ready product

Lesson Learned: Stitch Fix's approach demonstrates how GenAI can accelerate the Build-Measure-Learn cycle by rapidly generating new product ideas based on customer data, allowing for faster iteration and more targeted product development.

Potential Challenges and Considerations

While the integration of GenAI with Lean Startup principles offers exciting possibilities, it's important to consider potential challenges:

1. **Over-reliance on AI**: There's a risk of prioritizing AI-generated insights over human intuition and creativity.
2. **Data Quality and Bias**: GenAI systems are only as good as the data they're trained on. Poor quality or biased data can lead to flawed outputs.
3. **Ethical Considerations**: The use of AI raises questions about data privacy, transparency, and the potential displacement of human workers.
4. **Technical Barriers**: Implementing and maintaining advanced AI systems may require significant technical expertise and resources.

Case Study: Microsoft's Tay Chatbot

While not a startup example, Microsoft's experience with the Tay chatbot illustrates potential pitfalls of AI implementation.

Key Features:

1. Tay was an AI-powered chatbot designed to engage with people on Twitter
2. It was designed to learn and improve through interactions

Results:

- Within 24 hours of launch, Tay began posting offensive and inappropriate content
- Microsoft had to shut down the bot just 16 hours after its launch

Lesson Learned: This case highlights the importance of careful testing, monitoring, and ethical considerations when implementing AI systems, especially those that learn from user interactions.

Conclusion

The convergence of Lean Startup methodology and Generative AI represents a new frontier in entrepreneurship and innovation. By enhancing our ability to build, measure, and learn at unprecedented speeds, this combination has the potential to dramatically reduce the time and resources needed to achieve product-market fit and scale successful businesses.

GenAI can supercharge each aspect of the Lean Startup process - from generating and testing business hypotheses, to creating and iterating MVPs, to analyzing vast amounts of customer data for insights. It offers tools to accelerate decision-making, automate time-consuming tasks, and uncover patterns and opportunities that might be invisible to the human eye.

However, as we've seen, this powerful combination also comes with challenges. Entrepreneurs must navigate issues of data quality, ethical considerations, and the risk of over-reliance on AI-generated insights. The key to success will lie in finding the right balance - using GenAI to augment and accelerate human creativity and decision-making, rather than replace it entirely.

As we move forward, those who can effectively harness the power of GenAI while staying true to the core principles of the Lean Startup methodology - customer focus, rapid iteration, and data-driven decision making - will be well-positioned to lead the next wave of innovation and entrepreneurial success.

Key Takeaways:

1. GenAI can enhance core Lean Startup principles by accelerating hypothesis generation and testing, improving measurement and analysis, and speeding up MVP creation and iteration.
2. The Build-Measure-Learn cycle can be dramatically accelerated with GenAI, allowing for faster product development, more comprehensive data analysis, and quicker learning and iteration.
3. Real-world applications, like Airbnb's pricing algorithm and Stitch Fix's hybrid design process, demonstrate the potential of AI to enhance Lean Startup practices.
4. Challenges in implementing GenAI in a Lean Startup framework include risks of over-reliance on AI, data quality issues, ethical considerations, and technical barriers.
5. Success lies in finding the right balance between leveraging AI capabilities and maintaining the human-centric, customer-focused approach that is central to the Lean Startup methodology.
6. As GenAI tools become more accessible and powerful, understanding how to effectively integrate them into Lean Startup practices will become a crucial skill for entrepreneurs and innovators.

"Business model innovation is the new strategic imperative."
- Yves Pigneur

Chapter 5: AI-Enhanced Lean Canvas and Business Model Generation

Introduction

In the previous chapters, we explored the fundamentals of the Lean Startup methodology and the transformative potential of Generative AI. We then examined how these two powerful concepts converge to revolutionize the startup process. Now, we turn our attention to one of the most critical aspects of building a startup: creating and refining the business model.

The Lean Canvas, an adaptation of the Business Model Canvas by Ash Maurya, has become a staple tool for entrepreneurs to quickly outline and iterate on their business ideas. It encapsulates the essence of a startup's value proposition, customer segments, revenue streams, and other key elements on a single page. But what if we could supercharge this process with the power of AI?

In this chapter, we'll explore how Generative AI and machine learning can enhance the process of business model generation and refinement. From automated market research to AI-powered value proposition design, we'll uncover how these technologies can help entrepreneurs make more informed decisions, identify opportunities faster, and create more robust business models. Let's dive into this AI-enhanced approach to building the foundation of your startup.

1. Automated Market Research and Trend Analysis

One of the most time-consuming aspects of business model generation is conducting thorough market research. AI can significantly accelerate this process by:

- Analyzing vast amounts of online data to identify market trends
- Monitoring competitor activities and strategies
- Identifying emerging opportunities and potential threats

Case Study: CB Insights

CB Insights uses machine learning and natural language processing to analyze millions of data points and provide market intelligence.

Key Features:

1. AI-powered trend spotting across industries
2. Competitor tracking and analysis
3. Predictive analytics for emerging technologies and market shifts

Results:

- Used by 17 of the top 25 global tech companies
- Helped identify unicorn companies before they reached $1 billion valuations
- Provides insights that have informed over $1 trillion in M&A transactions

Lesson Learned: AI-powered market research tools can provide startups with enterprise-level market intelligence, helping them make more informed decisions about their business models and strategies.

2. AI-Powered Value Proposition Design

Crafting a compelling value proposition is crucial for any startup. AI can assist in this process by:

- Analyzing successful value propositions in similar markets
- Generating and testing multiple value proposition variations
- Predicting customer responses to different value propositions

Case Study: Persado

Persado uses AI to generate, analyze, and optimize marketing language, including value propositions.

Key Features:

1. AI-generated language across different emotions, features, and formats
2. Predictive analytics on the performance of different message elements
3. Continuous learning and optimization based on real-world results

Results:

- Clients have seen an average of 41% lift in marketing campaign performance
- Used by leading brands like JP Morgan Chase, Vodafone, and Dell
- Generated over 100 billion message permutations across industries

Lesson Learned: AI can significantly enhance the process of crafting and refining value propositions, leading to more effective communication with potential customers.

3. Intelligent Customer Segment Identification

Identifying and understanding customer segments is a critical part of building a successful business model. AI can enhance this process by:

- Analyzing large datasets to identify distinct customer groups
- Predicting customer behaviors and preferences
- Continuously refining customer segments based on real-world data

Case Study: Dynamic Yield (acquired by McDonald's)

Dynamic Yield uses AI to help companies personalize customer experiences across various touchpoints.

Key Features:

1. AI-powered customer segmentation
2. Real-time personalization of digital experiences
3. Predictive analytics for customer behavior

Results:

- Acquired by McDonald's in 2019 for over $300 million

- Helped increase McDonald's average check size in drive-thrus
- Used by brands like IKEA, Lacoste, and Ocado for personalization

Lesson Learned: AI-powered customer segmentation can help startups identify and target their most valuable customers more effectively, leading to more efficient use of resources and higher conversion rates.

4. Automated Financial Projections and Break-Even Analysis

Financial projections and break-even analysis are crucial for understanding the viability of a business model. AI can assist by:

- Generating financial models based on industry benchmarks and company data
- Performing sensitivity analyses to identify key financial drivers
- Continuously updating projections based on real-time data

Case Study: Fintopia

Fintopia uses AI to automate financial modeling and analysis for startups and small businesses.

Key Features:

1. AI-generated financial models and projections
2. Automated break-even analysis
3. Real-time updates based on actual financial data

Results:

- Used by thousands of startups across various industries
- Reduced time spent on financial modeling by up to 90%
- Helped startups raise over $500 million in funding

Lesson Learned: AI-powered financial modeling tools can help startups create more accurate and dynamic financial projections, enabling better decision-making and more effective communication with investors.

Potential Challenges and Considerations

While AI offers powerful enhancements to the business model generation process, it's important to consider potential challenges:

1. **Data Quality and Availability**: AI models are only as good as the data they're trained on. Startups in niche or emerging markets may face challenges with limited data availability.
2. **Over-reliance on AI**: There's a risk of blindly following AI-generated insights without applying human judgment and industry expertise.
3. **Cost and Technical Expertise**: Implementing advanced AI tools may require significant investment and technical know-how, which could be challenging for early-stage startups.
4. **Ethical Considerations**: The use of AI in analyzing customer data and behavior raises important questions about privacy and data ethics.

Conclusion

The integration of AI into the Lean Canvas and business model generation process represents a significant leap forward for startup entrepreneurs. By leveraging AI for market research, value proposition design, customer segmentation, and financial projections, startups can make more informed decisions, iterate faster, and build more robust business models.

From CB Insights' market intelligence to Persado's AI-generated value propositions, Dynamic Yield's customer segmentation, and Fintopia's automated financial modeling, we've seen how AI is already transforming various aspects of the business model generation process. These tools allow startups to operate with a level of insight and efficiency previously available only to large enterprises with significant resources.

However, it's crucial to remember that AI is a tool to augment human creativity and decision-making, not replace it. The most successful startups will be those that can effectively combine AI-generated insights with human expertise, industry knowledge, and entrepreneurial intuition.

As we move forward, the ability to leverage AI in business model generation and refinement will likely become a key competitive advantage for startups. Those who can master this integration will be well-positioned to identify opportunities faster, adapt to market changes more effectively, and ultimately build more successful and resilient businesses.

Key Takeaways:

1. AI can significantly enhance market research and trend analysis, providing startups with enterprise-level market intelligence.
2. AI-powered tools can assist in crafting and testing value propositions, leading to more effective communication with potential customers.
3. Intelligent customer segmentation powered by AI can help startups identify and target their most valuable customers more efficiently.
4. AI-driven financial modeling tools can create more accurate and dynamic financial projections, aiding in decision-making and investor communications.
5. While powerful, AI tools come with challenges including data quality issues, the risk of over-reliance on AI, and ethical considerations.
6. The most successful approach combines AI-generated insights with human expertise and entrepreneurial intuition.

7. Mastering AI-enhanced business model generation can provide a significant competitive advantage for startups in the rapidly evolving business landscape.

"If you are not embarrassed by the first version of your product, you've launched too late."
- Reid Hoffman

Chapter 6: Rapid Prototyping and MVP Development with AI

Introduction

In our journey through the convergence of Lean Startup methodologies and AI, we've explored how artificial intelligence can enhance business model generation and refine our understanding of market dynamics. Now, we turn our attention to a critical phase in any startup's life: the development of prototypes and Minimum Viable Products (MVPs).

The ability to rapidly prototype and iterate on MVPs is at the heart of the Lean Startup methodology. It allows entrepreneurs to test their hypotheses quickly and efficiently, gathering valuable user feedback without over-investing in unproven ideas. But what if we could make this process even faster and more effective?

In this chapter, we'll delve into how AI is revolutionizing the prototyping and MVP development process. From idea validation to automated code generation, from feature prioritization to AI-powered usability testing, we'll explore how these technologies are enabling startups to move from concept to market-ready product at unprecedented speeds. We'll pay special attention to groundbreaking platforms like XamunAI, which are redefining what's possible in rapid MVP development. Let's dive into this AI-powered future of product development.

1. AI-Assisted Idea Validation and Prioritization

Before diving into development, it's crucial to validate ideas and prioritize which ones to pursue. AI can assist in this process by:

- Analyzing market trends and consumer behavior data
- Simulating potential user reactions to different ideas
- Prioritizing ideas based on predicted market impact and feasibility

Case Study: Zest AI

While primarily known for its work in credit underwriting, Zest AI's machine learning platform has been used for idea validation in various industries.

Key Features:

1. Uses machine learning to analyze vast amounts of data
2. Provides insights on market trends and consumer preferences
3. Helps predict the potential success of new ideas

Results:

- Helped companies increase approval rates by up to 15%
- Reduced losses by up to 30% in various applications

- Enabled faster decision-making in idea selection and prioritization

Lesson Learned: AI can significantly enhance the idea validation process by providing data-driven insights, helping startups focus their resources on the most promising concepts.

2. Automated Code Generation for Quick Prototypes

Once an idea is validated, the next step is to create a prototype. AI is making this process faster and more efficient through automated code generation:

- Translating high-level descriptions into functional code
- Generating boilerplate code for common functionalities
- Suggesting optimizations and best practices

Case Study: GitHub Copilot

GitHub Copilot, developed by GitHub and OpenAI, is an AI pair programmer that helps developers write code faster.

Key Features:

1. Suggests whole lines or blocks of code as you type
2. Works with a variety of programming languages
3. Learns from the context of your project

Results:

- Users accept an average of 26% of Copilot's suggestions
- 60-75% of users report feeling more fulfilled with their work when using Copilot
- Significant reduction in time spent on boilerplate and repetitive coding tasks

Lesson Learned: AI-powered code generation tools can significantly speed up the prototyping process, allowing developers to focus on higher-level problem-solving and creative tasks.

3. Intelligent Feature Prioritization for MVPs

Deciding which features to include in an MVP is crucial. AI can assist in this process by:

- Analyzing user behavior data to predict feature importance
- Simulating user interactions with different feature sets
- Optimizing feature sets based on development time and potential impact

Case Study: Amplitude

Amplitude uses machine learning to help companies understand user behavior and prioritize features.

Key Features:

1. AI-powered user behavior analysis
2. Predictive analytics for feature impact
3. Automated insights generation

Results:

- Used by companies like Microsoft, Ford, and Twitter
- Helped companies increase conversion rates by up to 40%
- Enabled data-driven decisions on feature prioritization

Lesson Learned: AI can help startups make more informed decisions about which features to prioritize in their MVPs, leading to products that better meet user needs and market demands.

4. AI-Powered Usability Testing and User Feedback Analysis

Once a prototype or MVP is developed, AI can assist in testing and refining it:

- Simulating user interactions to identify potential usability issues
- Analyzing user feedback at scale to identify common themes and priorities
- Providing real-time suggestions for improvements based on user behavior

Case Study: UserTesting

UserTesting has incorporated AI into its platform to enhance usability testing and feedback analysis.

Key Features:

1. AI-powered analysis of user test videos
2. Automated insight generation from user feedback
3. Sentiment analysis of user comments

Results:

- Used by over 50% of the world's top 100 brands
- Reduced time to insight by up to 60%
- Increased team efficiency in analyzing user feedback by up to 70%

Lesson Learned: AI can significantly enhance the efficiency and effectiveness of usability testing and user feedback analysis, allowing startups to iterate on their MVPs more quickly and accurately.

5. XamunAI: Redefining Rapid MVP Development

XamunAI represents a significant leap forward in AI-assisted MVP development, showcasing the potential of AI to dramatically accelerate the entire process.

Key Features:

1. End-to-end AI-assisted development platform
2. High-fidelity MVP generation in under 6 weeks
3. Scalable architecture ensuring quality and future growth

Results:

- Reduces MVP development time from 4-6 months to under 6 weeks
- Enables rapid iteration based on market feedback
- Maintains high quality and scalability for future growth

Lesson Learned: Platforms like XamunAI demonstrate how AI can transform the entire MVP development process, allowing startups to move from concept to market-ready product at unprecedented speeds without sacrificing quality or scalability.

Potential Challenges and Considerations

While AI offers tremendous benefits in rapid prototyping and MVP development, it's important to consider potential challenges:

1. **Over-reliance on AI**: There's a risk of losing the human touch in product development, which is crucial for creating truly innovative and user-centric products.
2. **Data Privacy and Security**: As AI systems process vast amounts of data, ensuring the privacy and security of user information becomes increasingly important.

3. **Skill Gap**: Effectively utilizing AI-powered development tools may require new skills, potentially creating a learning curve for development teams.
4. **Cost Considerations**: While AI can speed up development, the initial investment in AI tools and platforms may be significant for some startups.

Conclusion

The integration of AI into rapid prototyping and MVP development represents a paradigm shift in how startups can bring their ideas to market. From idea validation with platforms like Zest AI, to automated code generation with GitHub Copilot, intelligent feature prioritization with Amplitude, and enhanced usability testing with UserTesting, AI is revolutionizing every stage of the development process.

The case of XamunAI particularly highlights the transformative potential of AI in this space. By enabling the development of high-fidelity MVPs in a fraction of the traditional time, while maintaining quality and scalability, platforms like XamunAI are redefining what's possible in rapid product development.

However, it's crucial to remember that AI is a tool to augment human creativity and expertise, not replace it. The most successful startups will be those that can effectively combine AI-powered tools with human insight, empathy, and innovation.

As we move forward, the ability to leverage AI in prototyping and MVP development will likely become a key competitive advantage for startups. Those who can master this integration will be well-positioned to bring products to market faster, iterate more efficiently, and ultimately build more successful and user-centric solutions.

Key Takeaways:

1. AI can significantly enhance idea validation and prioritization, helping startups focus on the most promising concepts.
2. Automated code generation tools can speed up the prototyping process, allowing developers to focus on higher-level tasks.
3. AI-powered feature prioritization can help startups create MVPs that better meet user needs and market demands.
4. AI enhances usability testing and user feedback analysis, enabling faster and more accurate product iterations.
5. Platforms like XamunAI demonstrate how AI can dramatically accelerate the entire MVP development process, reducing time-to-market from months to weeks.
6. While powerful, AI tools in MVP development come with challenges including the risk of over-reliance on AI, data privacy concerns, and potential skill gaps.
7. The most effective approach combines AI-powered tools with human creativity, empathy, and innovation.
8. Mastering AI-enhanced prototyping and MVP development can provide a significant competitive advantage in the fast-paced startup ecosystem.

"The only way to win is to learn faster than anyone else."
- Eric Ries

Chapter 7: Optimizing the Build-Measure-Learn Cycle with AI

Introduction

In our exploration of the synergy between Lean Startup methodologies and AI, we've seen how artificial intelligence can enhance business model generation, market research, and MVP development. Now, we turn our attention to the heart of the Lean Startup approach: the Build-Measure-Learn cycle.

This iterative process of building products, measuring their performance, and learning from the results is what drives continuous improvement and innovation in startups. But in today's fast-paced, data-rich environment, manually executing this cycle can be overwhelming and time-consuming.

Enter AI. By leveraging the power of machine learning and advanced analytics, we can supercharge each phase of the Build-Measure-Learn cycle. From automating A/B testing to providing real-time insights on user behavior, from supporting critical pivot-or-persevere decisions to aggregating learnings across multiple iterations, AI has the potential to make this cycle faster, more accurate, and more insightful than ever before.

In this chapter, we'll explore how AI is optimizing each stage of the Build-Measure-Learn cycle, illustrated with real-world case studies. Let's dive into this AI-powered revolution in startup methodology.

1. Automated A/B Testing Design and Analysis

A/B testing is a cornerstone of data-driven decision making in startups. AI can enhance this process by:

- Automatically generating test variants based on past performance data
- Optimizing test design for statistical significance
- Analyzing results in real-time and providing actionable insights

Case Study: Optimizely

Optimizely, a leading experimentation platform, has incorporated AI to enhance its A/B testing capabilities.

Key Features:

1. AI-powered experiment creation and targeting
2. Automated statistical analysis
3. Real-time results and recommendations

Results:

- Increased experiment velocity by up to 300%

- Improved win rates of experiments by up to 80%
- Used by companies like IBM, Microsoft, and eBay

Lesson Learned: AI can significantly enhance the efficiency and effectiveness of A/B testing, allowing startups to make data-driven decisions faster and with greater confidence.

2. Real-time User Behavior Tracking and Insights

Understanding user behavior is crucial for product improvement. AI can provide deeper, real-time insights by:

- Analyzing user interactions across multiple touchpoints
- Identifying patterns and anomalies in user behavior
- Providing real-time recommendations for product improvements

Case Study: Mixpanel

Mixpanel uses AI to provide advanced analytics and user behavior insights.

Key Features:

1. AI-powered user behavior analysis
2. Predictive analytics for user actions
3. Automated insights and anomaly detection

Results:

- Used by over 26,000 companies including Uber and Twitter
- Helped companies increase conversion rates by up to 24%
- Reduced time to insight by up to 80%

Lesson Learned: AI-powered analytics can provide startups with deeper, more actionable insights into user behavior, enabling faster and more effective product iterations.

3. AI-Driven Pivot or Persevere Decision Support

One of the most critical decisions in the Lean Startup process is whether to pivot or persevere with a current strategy. AI can support this decision-making process by:

- Analyzing multiple data points to assess product-market fit
- Simulating potential outcomes of different pivot strategies
- Providing data-driven recommendations based on historical patterns

Case Study: CBInsights

While primarily known for market intelligence, CBInsights' AI platform has been used by startups and VCs to inform pivot decisions.

Key Features:

1. AI-powered market trend analysis
2. Competitor tracking and benchmarking
3. Predictive analytics for market opportunities

Results:

- Used by top VCs and Fortune 500 companies
- Helped identify market shifts and opportunities for pivots
- Increased decision-making confidence for strategic shifts

Lesson Learned: AI can provide valuable, data-driven insights to support the critical pivot or persevere decision, helping startups make more informed strategic choices.

4. Intelligent Learning Aggregation and Knowledge Management

Effectively capturing and utilizing learnings from each iteration is crucial for long-term success. AI can enhance this process by:

- Automatically aggregating insights from multiple experiments and data sources
- Identifying patterns and connections across different learnings
- Suggesting applications of past learnings to new situations

Case Study: Tettra

Tettra, a knowledge management platform, has incorporated AI to enhance its capabilities.

Key Features:

1. AI-powered content organization and suggestion
2. Automated knowledge gap identification
3. Intelligent search and retrieval of information

Results:

- Used by companies like Shopify and InVision
- Reduced time spent searching for information by up to 35%
- Improved knowledge sharing and utilization across teams

Lesson Learned: AI can significantly enhance a startup's ability to capture, organize, and utilize learnings from each iteration of the Build-Measure-Learn cycle, leading to more effective knowledge management and decision-making.

Potential Challenges and Considerations

While AI offers powerful enhancements to the Build-Measure-Learn cycle, it's important to consider potential challenges:

1. **Data Quality and Quantity**: AI systems require large amounts of high-quality data to function effectively. Early-stage startups may struggle to generate sufficient data.
2. **Over reliance on Automation**: There's a risk of over-trusting AI-generated insights and losing the human intuition that's crucial in entrepreneurship.
3. **Ethical Considerations**: As AI systems process vast amounts of user data, ensuring privacy and ethical use of this information becomes increasingly important.
4. **Integration Complexity**: Implementing AI systems across the entire Build-Measure-Learn cycle may require significant technical expertise and resources.

Conclusion

The integration of AI into the Build-Measure-Learn cycle represents a quantum leap in how startups can iterate and improve their products. From Optimizely's AI-enhanced A/B testing to Mixpanel's deep user behavior insights, from CBInsights' data-driven pivot support to Tettra's intelligent knowledge management, we've seen how AI can enhance every stage of this crucial process.

By leveraging AI, startups can make their Build-Measure-Learn cycles faster, more accurate, and more insightful. This can lead to quicker iterations, more effective product improvements, and ultimately, a higher chance of achieving product-market fit and business success.

However, it's crucial to remember that AI is a tool to augment human decision-making, not replace it. The most successful startups will be those that can effectively combine AI-powered insights with human creativity, intuition, and domain expertise.

As we move forward, the ability to leverage AI in optimizing the Build-Measure-Learn cycle will likely become a key competitive advantage for startups. Those who can master this integration will be well-positioned to innovate faster, adapt more effectively to market changes, and ultimately build more successful and impactful businesses.

Key Takeaways:

1. AI can significantly enhance A/B testing processes, increasing experiment velocity and improving win rates.
2. AI-powered analytics provide deeper, real-time insights into user behavior, enabling faster and more effective product iterations.
3. AI can support critical pivot or persevere decisions by providing data-driven insights and predictive analytics.
4. Intelligent knowledge management systems powered by AI can help startups more effectively capture and utilize learnings from each iteration.
5. While powerful, AI tools in the Build-Measure-Learn cycle come with challenges including data requirements, the risk of over reliance on automation, and ethical considerations.
6. The most effective approach combines AI-powered insights with human creativity, intuition, and domain expertise.
7. Mastering AI-enhanced Build-Measure-Learn cycles can provide a significant competitive advantage in the fast-paced startup ecosystem.

"Get out of the building."
- Steve Blank

Chapter 8: AI-Powered Customer Discovery and Validation

Introduction

In our journey through the AI-enhanced Lean Startup methodology, we've explored how artificial intelligence can optimize various aspects of building and running a startup. From business model generation to rapid prototyping and the Build-Measure-Learn cycle, AI has shown its potential to revolutionize startup practices. Now, we turn our attention to one of the most critical aspects of any startup's success: understanding and validating customers.

Customer discovery and validation are at the heart of the Lean Startup approach. They involve identifying potential customers, understanding their needs, and verifying that your product or service meets those needs. Traditionally, this process has been time-consuming and often subjective. However, with the advent of

AI technologies, we now have powerful tools to make this process more efficient, data-driven, and insightful.

In this chapter, we'll explore how AI is transforming customer discovery and validation. From automating interview analysis to generating sophisticated customer personas, from conducting sentiment analysis to identifying early adopters, we'll see how AI is enabling startups to gain deeper customer insights faster than ever before. Let's dive into this AI-powered revolution in customer understanding.

1. Automated Customer Interview Transcription and Analysis

Customer interviews are a goldmine of information, but manually transcribing and analyzing them can be time-consuming. AI can streamline this process by:

- Automatically transcribing audio interviews to text
- Analyzing transcripts to identify key themes and insights
- Summarizing findings across multiple interviews

Case Study: Otter.ai

Otter.ai is an AI-powered transcription and analysis tool that has gained popularity among businesses for customer research.

Key Features:

1. Real-time transcription of audio to text
2. Automated identification of speakers
3. AI-powered summary and keyword extraction

Results:

- Used by over 10 million users worldwide
- Increased productivity in interview analysis by up to 30%

- Adopted by major companies like IBM and Dropbox for various transcription needs

Lesson Learned: AI-powered transcription and analysis tools can significantly speed up the customer interview process, allowing startups to derive insights faster and conduct more comprehensive research.

2. Sentiment Analysis of Customer Feedback

Understanding the emotional tone of customer feedback is crucial for product improvement. AI can provide deeper insights by:

- Analyzing text feedback for positive, negative, or neutral sentiment
- Identifying specific product features or aspects mentioned in feedback
- Tracking sentiment trends over time

Case Study: MonkeyLearn

MonkeyLearn offers AI-powered text analysis tools, including sentiment analysis, that have been used by startups for customer feedback analysis.

Key Features:

1. Customizable sentiment analysis models
2. Integration with various data sources (social media, surveys, etc.)
3. Real-time sentiment dashboards

Results:

- Used by companies like Drift and Uber
- Increased efficiency in feedback analysis by up to 50%
- Improved accuracy in sentiment classification by up to 85%

Lesson Learned: AI-powered sentiment analysis can provide startups with a more nuanced and comprehensive understanding of customer feedback, enabling more targeted product improvements.

3. AI-Powered Customer Persona Generation and Refinement

Creating accurate customer personas is essential for targeted marketing and product development. AI can enhance this process by:

- Analyzing large datasets to identify distinct customer groups
- Generating detailed persona profiles based on behavioral and demographic data
- Continuously refining personas based on new data

Case Study: Personas by Autopilot

Autopilot's Personas feature uses machine learning to automatically generate and update customer personas.

Key Features:

1. Automated persona generation based on customer data
2. Real-time persona updates as new data comes in
3. Integration with marketing automation tools

Results:

- Used by over 2,500 companies worldwide
- Reduced time spent on persona creation by up to 80%
- Improved marketing campaign performance by up to 25% through more accurate targeting

Lesson Learned: AI-powered persona generation can provide startups with more accurate and dynamic customer profiles, enabling more effective marketing and product development strategies.

4. Intelligent Identification of Early Adopters and Evangelists

Identifying and nurturing relationships with early adopters and potential evangelists is crucial for startup growth. AI can assist in this process by:

- Analyzing user behavior patterns to identify highly engaged users
- Predicting which users are most likely to become evangelists
- Recommending personalized engagement strategies for potential evangelists

Case Study: Insider

Insider is a multi-channel marketing platform that uses AI to help businesses identify and engage with their most valuable customers.

Key Features:

1. AI-powered predictive audience segmentation
2. Automated identification of high-value customers and potential evangelists
3. Personalized engagement recommendations

Results:

- Used by over 800 global brands, including Samsung and Uniqlo
- Increased customer lifetime value by up to 3x for some clients
- Improved customer retention rates by up to 87%

Lesson Learned: AI can help startups more effectively identify and engage with early adopters and potential evangelists, crucial for driving growth in the early stages of a startup.

Potential Challenges and Considerations

While AI offers powerful enhancements to customer discovery and validation, it's important to consider potential challenges:

1. **Data Privacy and Ethics**: As AI systems process vast amounts of customer data, ensuring privacy and ethical use of this information is crucial.
2. **Bias in AI Models**: AI models can inadvertently perpetuate or amplify biases present in training data, potentially leading to skewed customer insights.
3. **Over reliance on AI Insights**: There's a risk of over-trusting AI-generated insights and losing the nuanced understanding that comes from direct customer interaction.
4. **Integration and Technical Expertise**: Implementing sophisticated AI tools may require significant technical expertise and resources, which can be challenging for early-stage startups.

Conclusion

The integration of AI into customer discovery and validation processes represents a significant advancement in how startups can understand and serve their customers. From Otter.ai's interview transcription capabilities to MonkeyLearn's sentiment analysis, from Autopilot's dynamic persona generation to Insider's intelligent early adopter identification, we've seen how AI can enhance every stage of customer understanding.

By leveraging AI, startups can gain deeper customer insights faster and more accurately than ever before. This can lead to more targeted product development, more effective marketing strategies, and ultimately, a higher chance of achieving product-market fit and business success.

However, it's crucial to remember that AI is a tool to augment human understanding, not replace it. The most successful startups will be those that can effectively combine AI-powered insights with human empathy, intuition, and direct customer engagement.

As we move forward, the ability to leverage AI in customer discovery and validation will likely become a key competitive advantage for startups. Those who can master this integration will be well-positioned to understand their customers better, adapt more quickly to changing needs, and ultimately build more customer-centric and successful businesses.

Key Takeaways:

1. AI can significantly speed up and enhance the customer interview process through automated transcription and analysis.
2. AI-powered sentiment analysis provides a more nuanced and comprehensive understanding of customer feedback.
3. Automated, AI-driven customer persona generation enables more accurate and dynamic customer profiling.
4. AI can help identify and engage early adopters and potential evangelists more effectively.
5. While powerful, AI tools in customer discovery come with challenges including data privacy concerns, potential biases, and the risk of over reliance on automated insights.
6. The most effective approach combines AI-powered insights with human empathy and direct customer engagement.
7. Mastering AI-enhanced customer discovery and validation can provide a significant competitive advantage in understanding and serving customers.

"Growth is never by mere chance; it is the result of forces working together."
- James Cash Penney

Chapter 9: AI-Driven Growth Hacking and Marketing Strategies

Introduction

As we've journeyed through the AI-enhanced Lean Startup methodology, we've explored how artificial intelligence can revolutionize various aspects of building and running a startup. From business model generation to rapid prototyping, from optimizing the Build-Measure-Learn cycle to enhancing customer discovery and validation, AI has demonstrated its potential to transform startup practices. Now, we turn our attention to a critical challenge that every startup faces: achieving rapid and sustainable growth.

Growth hacking, a term coined by Sean Ellis in 2010, refers to the use of creative, low-cost strategies to help businesses acquire and retain customers. When combined with traditional marketing approaches, growth hacking can be a powerful tool for startups to scale quickly. But in today's data-rich, fast-paced digital landscape, manually executing these strategies can be overwhelming and time-consuming.

Enter AI. By leveraging machine learning, natural language processing, and advanced analytics, we can supercharge our growth hacking and marketing efforts. From automating content creation to optimizing social media strategies, from managing ad campaigns to predicting customer behavior, AI has the potential to make our growth efforts more efficient, targeted, and effective than ever before.

In this chapter, we'll explore how AI is transforming growth hacking and marketing strategies, illustrated with real-world case studies. Let's dive into this AI-powered revolution in startup growth.

1. Automated Content Generation for Various Channels

Content creation is a crucial part of any marketing strategy, but it can be time-consuming. AI can assist by:

- Generating blog posts, social media updates, and email content
- Creating personalized content for different audience segments
- Optimizing content for SEO and readability

Case Study: Jasper (formerly Jarvis)

Jasper is an AI-powered content creation platform that has gained popularity among marketers and entrepreneurs.

Key Features:

1. AI-generated content for various formats (blog posts, ads, emails)
2. Templates for different content types
3. SEO optimization features

Results:

- Used by over 50,000 teams worldwide
- Increased content production speed by up to 5x for some users
- Helped companies increase organic traffic by up to 300%

Lesson Learned: AI-powered content generation can significantly speed up the content creation process, allowing startups to maintain a consistent content schedule across multiple channels without sacrificing quality.

2. AI-Powered Social Media Strategy Optimization

Managing social media presence effectively is crucial for startups. AI can enhance this process by:

- Analyzing engagement patterns to determine optimal posting times
- Suggesting content topics likely to resonate with the audience
- Automating responses to common customer queries

Case Study: Hootsuite Insights Powered by Brandwatch

Hootsuite, a popular social media management platform, integrates AI-powered insights through its partnership with Brandwatch.

Key Features:

1. AI-driven social listening and trend analysis
2. Automated sentiment analysis of social mentions

3. Predictive analytics for content performance

Results:

- Used by over 18 million users worldwide
- Increased social engagement rates by up to 40% for some clients
- Reduced time spent on social media management by up to 30%

Lesson Learned: AI can help startups optimize their social media strategies by providing data-driven insights, allowing for more effective audience engagement and brand building.

3. Intelligent Ad Campaign Management and Optimization

Effective advertising is key to startup growth, but managing campaigns can be complex. AI can assist by:

- Automatically adjusting bid strategies based on real-time performance data
- Creating and testing multiple ad variations
- Optimizing ad targeting based on user behavior and characteristics

Case Study: Albert.ai

Albert.ai is an autonomous AI marketing platform that manages and optimizes digital advertising campaigns.

Key Features:

1. Autonomous campaign management across multiple channels
2. Real-time budget allocation and bid adjustments
3. Automated A/B testing of ad creative and targeting

Results:

- Increased return on ad spend by up to 40% for some clients
- Reduced cost per acquisition by up to 30%
- Managed budgets of up to $300 million annually for large clients

Lesson Learned: AI-driven ad campaign management can significantly improve advertising effectiveness and efficiency, allowing startups to maximize their often limited marketing budgets.

4. Predictive Analytics for Customer Acquisition and Retention

Understanding and predicting customer behavior is crucial for sustainable growth. AI can help by:

- Identifying patterns in customer data to predict future behavior
- Segmenting customers based on likelihood to convert or churn
- Recommending personalized retention strategies for at-risk customers

Case Study: DataRobot

DataRobot is an AI-powered platform that helps businesses implement machine learning models, including for customer analytics.

Key Features:

1. Automated machine learning model creation
2. Predictive analytics for customer behavior
3. Integration with existing business intelligence tools

Results:

- Used by a third of the Fortune 50 companies
- Increased customer retention rates by up to 20% for some clients
- Improved accuracy of sales forecasts by up to 30%

Lesson Learned: AI-powered predictive analytics can help startups make more informed decisions about customer acquisition and retention strategies, leading to more efficient growth and higher customer lifetime value.

Potential Challenges and Considerations

While AI offers powerful enhancements to growth hacking and marketing strategies, it's important to consider potential challenges:

1. **Data Privacy and Compliance**: As AI systems process vast amounts of customer data, ensuring compliance with data protection regulations is crucial.
2. **Maintaining Brand Voice**: While AI can generate content quickly, ensuring it aligns with your brand voice and values can be challenging.
3. **Over reliance on Automation**: There's a risk of losing the creative, human touch that's often crucial in marketing and growth strategies.
4. **Technical Implementation**: Implementing sophisticated AI tools may require significant technical expertise and resources, which can be challenging for early-stage startups.

Conclusion

The integration of AI into growth hacking and marketing strategies represents a significant leap forward in how startups can acquire and retain customers. From Jasper's content generation capabilities to Hootsuite's AI-powered social media insights, from Albert.ai's intelligent ad campaign management to DataRobot's predictive analytics, we've seen how AI can enhance every aspect of a startup's growth efforts.

By leveraging AI, startups can execute more sophisticated, data-driven growth strategies that were once the domain of large enterprises with significant resources. This can lead to more efficient customer acquisition, more effective engagement, and ultimately, faster and more sustainable growth.

However, it's crucial to remember that AI is a tool to augment human creativity and strategy, not replace it. The most successful startups will be those that can effectively combine AI-powered insights and automation with human intuition, creativity, and authentic brand building.

As we move forward, the ability to leverage AI in growth hacking and marketing will likely become a key competitive advantage for startups. Those who can master this integration will be well-positioned to scale their businesses more efficiently, adapt more quickly to market changes, and ultimately build more successful and impactful companies.

Key Takeaways:

1. AI-powered content generation can significantly speed up content creation across multiple channels, enabling consistent and quality content marketing.
2. AI can optimize social media strategies by providing data-driven insights on posting times, content topics, and audience engagement.
3. Intelligent ad campaign management powered by AI can improve advertising effectiveness and efficiency, maximizing limited marketing budgets.
4. Predictive analytics driven by AI can enhance customer acquisition and retention strategies, leading to more sustainable growth.
5. While powerful, AI tools in growth hacking and marketing come with challenges including data privacy concerns,

maintaining brand voice, and the risk of over reliance on automation.
6. The most effective approach combines AI-powered insights and automation with human creativity and authentic brand building.
7. Mastering AI-enhanced growth strategies can provide a significant competitive advantage in the fast-paced startup ecosystem.

"What gets measured gets managed."
- Peter Drucker

Chapter 10: Lean Analytics with AI

Introduction

As we've journeyed through the AI-enhanced Lean Startup methodology, we've explored how artificial intelligence can revolutionize various aspects of building and scaling a startup. From business model generation to rapid prototyping, from customer discovery to growth hacking, AI has demonstrated its transformative potential. Now, we turn our attention to a critical aspect that underpins all of these areas: analytics.

Lean Analytics, a concept popularized by Alistair Croll and Benjamin Yoskovitz, emphasizes the importance of measuring and learning as you grow a startup. It's about finding the right metric to focus on at the right time. But in today's data-rich environment, identifying the most important metrics and deriving actionable insights can be overwhelming.

This is where AI comes in. By leveraging machine learning and advanced data analysis techniques, we can supercharge our analytics capabilities. From automated tracking and analysis of key metrics to real-time dashboards with AI-generated insights, from predictive modeling to intelligent benchmarking, AI has the potential to make our analytics more powerful, more accessible, and more actionable than ever before.

In this chapter, we'll explore how AI is transforming lean analytics, illustrated with real-world case studies. Let's dive into this AI-powered revolution in startup measurement and learning.

1. Automated Tracking and Analysis of Key Metrics

Tracking the right metrics is crucial for startup success, but it can be time-consuming and complex. AI can assist by:

- Automatically collecting and processing data from various sources
- Identifying the most relevant metrics for your current stage and business model
- Providing real-time analysis and alerts for significant changes in key metrics

Case Study: Mixpanel

Mixpanel is an advanced analytics platform that leverages AI to provide deeper insights into user behavior and business metrics.

Key Features:

1. Automatic event tracking and user flow analysis
2. AI-powered anomaly detection
3. Predictive analytics for user behavior

Results:

- Used by over 26,000 companies including Uber and Expedia
- Increased user engagement by up to 24% for some clients
- Reduced time spent on data analysis by up to 80%

Lesson Learned: AI-powered analytics platforms can significantly streamline the process of tracking and analyzing key metrics, allowing startups to focus on acting on insights rather than getting bogged down in data collection and processing.

2. Real-time Dashboards with AI-Generated Insights

Having data is one thing; understanding what it means and what to do about it is another. AI can help by:

- Creating dynamic, real-time dashboards that highlight the most important information
- Automatically generating insights and explanations for data trends
- Suggesting potential actions based on current metrics and historical data

Case Study: Sisense

Sisense is a business intelligence platform that uses AI to provide advanced analytics and insights.

Key Features:

1. AI-powered data preparation and modeling
2. Natural language query for data exploration
3. Automated insights generation

Results:

- Used by companies like Philips, Nasdaq, and Rolls-Royce
- Reduced time to insight by up to 50% for some clients

- Increased data utilization across organizations by up to 80%

Lesson Learned: AI can transform raw data into actionable insights in real-time, enabling startups to make faster, more informed decisions.

3. Predictive Modeling for Startup Growth Trajectories

Understanding potential future outcomes is crucial for strategic planning. AI can assist by:

- Analyzing historical data to identify growth patterns
- Creating predictive models for various business scenarios
- Continuously updating predictions based on new data

Case Study: DataRobot

DataRobot is an AI-powered platform that helps businesses implement machine learning models, including for predictive analytics.

Key Features:

1. Automated machine learning model creation
2. Time series forecasting
3. What-if analysis for different scenarios

Results:

- Used by a third of the Fortune 50 companies
- Improved forecast accuracy by up to 25% for some clients
- Reduced time spent on predictive modeling by up to 90%

Lesson Learned: AI-powered predictive modeling can provide startups with more accurate forecasts and scenario planning, enabling better strategic decision-making.

4. Intelligent Benchmarking Against Industry Standards

Understanding how you compare to industry standards and competitors is crucial. AI can help by:

- Automatically collecting and analyzing industry data
- Providing personalized benchmarks based on your startup's stage and sector
- Suggesting areas for improvement based on comparative analysis

Case Study: Craft.co

Craft.co uses AI to provide comprehensive company intelligence and benchmarking.

Key Features:

1. AI-powered data collection from millions of sources
2. Automated company comparisons and benchmarking
3. Personalized insights and recommendations

Results:

- Used by companies like Dell, Salesforce, and Deloitte
- Increased efficiency in competitive analysis by up to 70%
- Provided insights leading to strategic pivots for several startups

Lesson Learned: AI-driven benchmarking can provide startups with a clearer understanding of their position in the market and identify key areas for improvement.

Potential Challenges and Considerations

While AI offers powerful enhancements to lean analytics, it's important to consider potential challenges:

1. **Data Quality and Quantity**: AI systems require large amounts of high-quality data to function effectively. Early-stage startups may struggle to generate sufficient data.
2. **Over reliance on Metrics**: There's a risk of focusing too much on metrics and losing sight of qualitative factors that are crucial for startup success.
3. **Interpretation of AI Insights**: While AI can generate insights, interpreting them correctly and deciding on appropriate actions still requires human judgment.
4. **Cost and Technical Expertise**: Implementing sophisticated AI analytics tools may require significant investment and technical know-how.

Conclusion

The integration of AI into lean analytics represents a significant advancement in how startups can measure, learn, and make decisions. From Mixpanel's automated tracking and analysis to Sisense's AI-generated insights, from DataRobot's predictive modeling to Craft.co's intelligent benchmarking, we've seen how AI can enhance every aspect of startup analytics.

By leveraging AI, startups can gain deeper, more actionable insights faster than ever before. This can lead to more informed decision-making, more effective resource allocation, and ultimately, a higher chance of achieving sustainable growth and success.

However, it's crucial to remember that AI is a tool to augment human decision-making, not replace it. The most successful startups will be those that can effectively combine AI-powered analytics with human intuition, creativity, and deep understanding of their business and market.

As we move forward, the ability to leverage AI in lean analytics will likely become a key competitive advantage for startups. Those who can master this integration will be well-positioned to make better decisions, adapt more quickly to market changes, and ultimately build more successful and impactful businesses.

Key Takeaways:

1. AI can automate the tracking and analysis of key metrics, allowing startups to focus on acting on insights rather than data processing.
2. AI-powered dashboards can provide real-time, actionable insights, enabling faster and more informed decision-making.
3. Predictive modeling enhanced by AI can offer more accurate forecasts and scenario planning, supporting better strategic decisions.
4. AI-driven benchmarking can provide startups with a clearer understanding of their market position and areas for improvement.
5. While powerful, AI tools in analytics come with challenges including data requirements, the risk of metric obsession, and the need for human interpretation of AI-generated insights.
6. The most effective approach combines AI-powered analytics with human intuition and deep business understanding.
7. Mastering AI-enhanced lean analytics can provide a significant competitive advantage in the data-driven startup ecosystem.

"Accounting is the language of business."
- Warren Buffett

Chapter 11: AI for Agile Financial Management in Startups

Introduction

As we've progressed through our exploration of AI-enhanced Lean Startup methodologies, we've seen how artificial intelligence can revolutionize various aspects of building and scaling a startup. From customer discovery to growth hacking, and from lean analytics to product development, AI has demonstrated its transformative potential. Now, we turn our attention to a critical yet often challenging aspect of startup operations: financial management.

For many startups, financial management can be a daunting task. Limited resources, unpredictable cash flows, and the need for quick decision-making can make traditional financial management approaches insufficient. This is where the concept of agile financial management comes in, emphasizing flexibility, rapid iteration, and data-driven decision-making.

By integrating AI into agile financial management, startups can gain unprecedented insights into their financial health, make more accurate projections, and optimize their financial strategies in real-time. From automated burn rate calculations to AI-powered cash flow optimization, from intelligent pricing strategies to automated financial reporting, AI has the potential to transform how startups manage their finances.

In this chapter, we'll explore how AI is revolutionizing agile financial management for startups, illustrated with real-world case studies. Let's dive into this AI-powered financial revolution.

1. Automated Burn Rate Calculation and Runway Prediction

Understanding burn rate and predicting runway is crucial for startup survival. AI can enhance this process by:

- Automatically calculating burn rate based on real-time financial data
- Predicting future burn rates considering various factors and scenarios
- Providing early warnings when runway becomes critically short

Case Study: Pry

Pry is a financial planning software that uses AI to provide startups with insights into their burn rate and runway.

Key Features:

1. Real-time burn rate calculations
2. AI-powered runway predictions
3. Scenario modeling for different financial situations

Results:

- Used by over 500 startups
- Reduced time spent on financial modeling by up to 80%
- Helped startups extend their runway by an average of 3 months through better financial planning

Lesson Learned: AI-powered burn rate and runway prediction tools can provide startups with more accurate and timely insights into their financial sustainability, enabling proactive decision-making.

2. AI-Powered Cash Flow Optimization

Managing cash flow effectively is a common challenge for startups. AI can assist by:

- Predicting future cash inflows and outflows
- Suggesting optimal timing for payments and collections
- Identifying potential cash flow bottlenecks in advance

Case Study: Float

Float is an AI-enhanced cash flow forecasting tool designed for small businesses and startups.

Key Features:

1. AI-driven cash flow forecasting
2. Automated reconciliation with accounting software
3. Scenario planning for different financial decisions

Results:

- Used by over 3,000 businesses worldwide
- Improved cash flow forecasting accuracy by up to 40%
- Helped businesses save an average of 5 hours per week on cash flow management

Lesson Learned: AI can significantly improve the accuracy and efficiency of cash flow management, helping startups maintain financial stability and make better-informed financial decisions.

3. Intelligent Pricing Strategy Recommendations

Determining the right pricing strategy is crucial for startup success. AI can help by:

- Analyzing market data and competitor pricing
- Predicting customer willingness to pay for different segments
- Suggesting optimal pricing strategies based on business goals

Case Study: Perfect Price

Perfect Price is an AI-powered dynamic pricing platform that helps businesses optimize their pricing strategies.

Key Features:

1. AI-driven price optimization
2. Real-time market data analysis
3. Customized pricing strategies for different customer segments

Results:

- Used by companies like Zipcar and Uber
- Increased revenue by up to 15% for some clients
- Improved price perception among customers while maintaining profitability

Lesson Learned: AI-powered pricing tools can help startups find the optimal balance between competitiveness and profitability, leading to improved financial performance.

4. Automated Financial Reporting and Investor Updates

Preparing financial reports and investor updates can be time-consuming. AI can streamline this process by:

- Automatically generating financial reports from various data sources
- Creating visually appealing and easy-to-understand financial dashboards
- Drafting initial versions of investor update emails

Case Study: Fathom

Fathom is an AI-enhanced financial reporting and analysis tool designed for small businesses and startups.

Key Features:

1. Automated financial report generation
2. AI-powered financial analysis and insights
3. Customizable dashboards for different stakeholders

Results:

- Used by over 50,000 businesses worldwide
- Reduced time spent on financial reporting by up to 70%
- Improved financial literacy among non-financial stakeholders in organizations

Lesson Learned: AI can significantly reduce the time and effort required for financial reporting while improving the quality and accessibility of financial information for various stakeholders.

Potential Challenges and Considerations

While AI offers powerful enhancements to agile financial management, it's important to consider potential challenges:

1. **Data Security and Privacy**: Financial data is highly sensitive, and ensuring its security in AI systems is crucial.
2. **Regulatory Compliance**: AI systems need to be designed to comply with relevant financial regulations, which can be complex and vary by jurisdiction.
3. **Overreliance on AI**: There's a risk of overrelying on AI-generated financial insights without applying human judgment and industry expertise.
4. **Implementation Costs**: Sophisticated AI financial management tools can be expensive, which might be challenging for cash-strapped startups.

Conclusion

The integration of AI into agile financial management represents a significant advancement in how startups can manage their finances. From Pry's burn rate predictions to Float's cash flow optimization, from Perfect Price's intelligent pricing strategies to Fathom's automated reporting, we've seen how AI can enhance every aspect of startup financial management.

By leveraging AI, startups can gain deeper, more actionable financial insights faster than ever before. This can lead to more informed financial decision-making, more efficient use of resources, and ultimately, a higher chance of achieving sustainable growth and success.

However, it's crucial to remember that AI is a tool to augment human financial expertise, not replace it. The most successful startups will be those that can effectively combine AI-powered financial insights with human judgment, industry knowledge, and strategic thinking.

As we move forward, the ability to leverage AI in agile financial management will likely become a key competitive advantage for startups. Those who can master this integration will be well-positioned to make better financial decisions, adapt more quickly to market changes, and ultimately build more financially sustainable and successful businesses.

Key Takeaways:

1. AI can automate and enhance burn rate calculations and runway predictions, providing startups with more accurate insights into their financial sustainability.
2. AI-powered cash flow optimization tools can significantly improve the accuracy and efficiency of cash flow management.
3. Intelligent pricing tools leveraging AI can help startups find the optimal balance between competitiveness and profitability.
4. AI can streamline financial reporting and investor communication, saving time and improving the quality of financial information.
5. While powerful, AI tools in financial management come with challenges including data security concerns, regulatory compliance, and the risk of overreliance on AI-generated insights.
6. The most effective approach combines AI-powered financial tools with human expertise and strategic thinking.
7. Mastering AI-enhanced agile financial management can provide a significant competitive advantage in the startup ecosystem.

"The secret to successful fundraising is to have a great business and know how to tell your story."
- Marc Benioff

Chapter 12: AI-Assisted Pitch Deck and Investor Relations

Introduction

Throughout our exploration of AI-enhanced Lean Startup methodologies, we've seen how artificial intelligence can revolutionize various aspects of building and scaling a startup. From customer discovery to product development, from growth hacking to financial management, AI has demonstrated its transformative potential. Now, we turn our attention to a critical challenge that every startup faces: attracting investors and managing investor relations.

Creating a compelling pitch deck and effectively managing investor relationships are crucial skills for any startup founder. These tasks require a delicate balance of data-driven insights, storytelling, and relationship management. But in today's fast-paced, competitive startup ecosystem, manually crafting the perfect pitch and managing investor communications can be time-consuming and challenging.

This is where AI comes in. By leveraging machine learning, natural language processing, and data analytics, we can enhance our approach to pitch deck creation and investor relations. From AI-generated pitch deck content to intelligent investor matching, from automated due diligence preparation to AI-powered negotiation strategy recommendations, AI has the potential to make our investor-facing efforts more efficient, targeted, and effective than ever before.

In this chapter, we'll explore how AI is transforming pitch deck creation and investor relations, illustrated with real-world case studies. Let's dive into this AI-powered revolution in startup fundraising and investor management.

1. AI-Generated Pitch Deck Content and Design

Creating a compelling pitch deck is both an art and a science. AI can assist in this process by:

- Analyzing successful pitch decks to identify effective structures and content
- Generating initial drafts of pitch deck content based on startup data
- Suggesting design elements and layouts that resonate with investors

Case Study: Beautiful.ai

Beautiful.ai is an AI-powered presentation software that includes features specifically designed for creating pitch decks.

Key Features:

1. AI-driven slide design and layout suggestions
2. Smart templates for common pitch deck sections
3. Automated formatting and styling

Results:

- Used by teams at companies like Google, Netflix, and Spotify
- Reduced time spent on pitch deck creation by up to 50%
- Improved presentation quality scores in user surveys by 30%

Lesson Learned: AI-assisted pitch deck creation can significantly reduce the time and effort required to produce professional-quality presentations, allowing founders to focus more on refining their message and strategy.

2. Intelligent Investor Matching and Outreach

Finding the right investors for your startup is crucial. AI can enhance this process by:

- Analyzing investor portfolios and preferences to identify good matches
- Predicting investor interest based on historical data and current trends
- Optimizing outreach strategies for different investor profiles

Case Study: Affinity

Affinity is an AI-powered relationship intelligence platform used by venture capital firms and startups for investor matching and management.

Key Features:

1. AI-driven investor recommendations
2. Automated relationship mapping
3. Predictive analytics for investor interest

Results:

- Used by over 1,500 companies worldwide
- Increased successful investor matches by up to 35%
- Reduced time spent on investor research by up to 70%

Lesson Learned: AI can significantly improve the efficiency and effectiveness of investor targeting and outreach, helping startups connect with the most relevant potential investors.

3. Automated Due Diligence Preparation

Preparing for due diligence can be a time-consuming process. AI can assist by:

- Automatically organizing and categorizing relevant documents
- Identifying potential red flags or areas that need attention
- Generating initial drafts of common due diligence responses

Case Study: Diligend

Diligend is an AI-enhanced due diligence platform that automates much of the due diligence process.

Key Features:

1. AI-powered document analysis and organization
2. Automated questionnaire responses
3. Real-time collaboration tools for due diligence teams

Results:

- Used by major financial institutions and investment firms
- Reduced time spent on due diligence preparation by up to 60%
- Improved accuracy and completeness of due diligence responses

Lesson Learned: AI can streamline the due diligence process, helping startups present a more organized and thorough picture to potential investors while saving significant time and resources.

4. AI-Powered Negotiation Strategy Recommendations

Negotiating with investors requires skill and strategy. AI can support this process by:

- Analyzing historical deal data to suggest negotiation strategies
- Predicting potential investor concerns or objections
- Recommending optimal deal terms based on market conditions and startup stage

Case Study: Cognitiv+

While primarily focused on contract analysis, Cognitiv+ has been used by some startups and investors to enhance negotiation strategies.

Key Features:

1. AI-driven contract analysis
2. Identification of unusual or potentially unfavorable terms
3. Comparison with industry-standard terms and conditions

Results:

- Used by law firms and corporate legal departments worldwide

- Reduced time spent on contract review by up to 80%
- Improved identification of potential issues in investor agreements

Lesson Learned: AI can provide valuable insights and recommendations for negotiation strategies, helping startups secure more favorable investment terms.

Potential Challenges and Considerations

While AI offers powerful enhancements to pitch deck creation and investor relations, it's important to consider potential challenges:

1. **Maintaining Authenticity**: There's a risk of losing the unique voice and passion of the founders if relying too heavily on AI-generated content.
2. **Data Privacy and Confidentiality**: Handling sensitive business information in AI systems requires robust security measures.
3. **Overreliance on AI Recommendations**: While AI can provide valuable insights, human judgment is crucial in investor relations and negotiations.
4. **Technology Limitations**: AI may not fully understand nuanced industry contexts or cutting-edge innovations, potentially leading to oversimplified recommendations.

Conclusion

The integration of AI into pitch deck creation and investor relations represents a significant advancement in how startups can approach fundraising and investor management. From Beautiful.ai's pitch deck assistance to Affinity's investor matching, from Diligend's due diligence automation to Cognitiv+'s negotiation support, we've seen how AI can enhance every aspect of a startup's investor-facing efforts.

By leveraging AI, startups can create more compelling pitch decks, identify and connect with the most relevant investors, streamline due diligence processes, and negotiate more effectively. This can lead to more successful fundraising efforts, stronger investor relationships, and ultimately, better chances of startup success.

However, it's crucial to remember that AI is a tool to augment human creativity, judgment, and relationship-building skills, not replace them. The most successful startups will be those that can effectively combine AI-powered insights and automation with authentic storytelling, strategic thinking, and genuine relationship building.

As we move forward, the ability to leverage AI in pitch deck creation and investor relations will likely become a key competitive advantage for startups. Those who can master this integration will be well-positioned to attract the right investors, secure favorable terms, and build strong, lasting relationships with their financial partners.

Key Takeaways:

1. AI-assisted pitch deck creation can significantly reduce time spent on design while improving overall quality and effectiveness.
2. Intelligent investor matching powered by AI can help startups connect with the most relevant potential investors more efficiently.
3. AI can streamline due diligence preparation, saving time and improving the thoroughness of responses.
4. AI-powered negotiation support can provide valuable insights, potentially leading to more favorable investment terms.
5. While powerful, AI tools in investor relations come with challenges including maintaining authenticity, ensuring data privacy, and avoiding overreliance on AI recommendations.

6. The most effective approach combines AI-powered tools with human creativity, strategic thinking, and genuine relationship building.
7. Mastering AI-enhanced pitch deck creation and investor relations can provide a significant competitive advantage in the crowded startup funding landscape.

"Talent wins games, but teamwork and intelligence win championships."
- Michael Jordan

Chapter 13: AI for Lean Team Management and Collaboration

Introduction

As we've journeyed through the AI-enhanced Lean Startup methodology, we've explored how artificial intelligence can revolutionize various aspects of building and scaling a startup. From customer discovery to product development, from financial management to investor relations, AI has demonstrated its transformative potential. Now, we turn our attention to a critical internal aspect of every startup: team management and collaboration.

In the fast-paced, resource-constrained environment of a lean startup, effective team management and collaboration are crucial for success. However, traditional management approaches can often be too rigid or time-consuming for the dynamic needs of a startup. This is where AI can play a transformative role.

By leveraging machine learning, natural language processing, and predictive analytics, we can enhance our approach to team management and collaboration. From intelligent task allocation to AI-powered skill gap analysis, from automated meeting summaries to predictive analytics for team performance, AI has the potential to make our teams more efficient, adaptive, and effective than ever before.

In this chapter, we'll explore how AI is transforming lean team management and collaboration, illustrated with real-world case studies. Let's dive into this AI-powered revolution in startup team dynamics.

1. Intelligent Task Allocation and Workload Balancing

Efficiently allocating tasks and balancing workloads is crucial for lean teams. AI can assist by:

- Analyzing team members' skills, availability, and past performance
- Suggesting optimal task assignments based on project requirements
- Predicting potential bottlenecks and recommending workload adjustments

Case Study: Forecast

Forecast is an AI-powered project and resource management platform that includes intelligent task allocation features.

Key Features:

1. AI-driven task assignment recommendations
2. Automated workload balancing

3. Predictive analytics for project timelines and resource needs

Results:

- Used by over 40,000 users across 1,000+ companies
- Improved project delivery times by up to 20%
- Increased resource utilization by up to 30%

Lesson Learned: AI-assisted task allocation and workload balancing can significantly improve team efficiency and project outcomes in lean startup environments.

2. AI-Powered Team Skill Gap Analysis and Training Recommendations

Identifying skill gaps and providing appropriate training is essential for team growth. AI can enhance this process by:

- Analyzing team skills against project requirements
- Identifying current and future skill gaps
- Recommending personalized training programs for team members

Case Study: Degreed

Degreed is a skill-building platform that uses AI to provide personalized learning experiences and skill gap analysis.

Key Features:

1. AI-driven skill assessment and gap analysis
2. Personalized learning path recommendations
3. Integration with various learning content providers

Results:

- Used by organizations like Airbnb, Boeing, and Unilever

- Improved skill development rates by up to 50%
- Reduced time to proficiency for new skills by up to 30%

Lesson Learned: AI can help lean startups identify and address skill gaps more effectively, ensuring teams have the capabilities needed for current and future challenges.

3. Automated Meeting Summarization and Action Item Tracking

Efficient meetings and follow-ups are crucial for lean teams. AI can assist by:

- Transcribing and summarizing meetings in real-time
- Extracting key action items and decisions
- Tracking follow-ups and reminding team members of pending tasks

Case Study: Otter.ai

Otter.ai is an AI-powered conversation intelligence platform that offers real-time transcription and meeting summarization.

Key Features:

1. Real-time meeting transcription and note-taking
2. Automated summary generation
3. Action item extraction and assignment

Results:

- Used by over 10 million users worldwide
- Reduced time spent on meeting follow-ups by up to 40%
- Improved meeting productivity and accountability

Lesson Learned: AI-powered meeting tools can help lean startups save time, improve communication, and ensure better follow-through on action items.

4. Predictive Analytics for Team Performance and Burnout Prevention

Maintaining team performance while preventing burnout is a delicate balance. AI can help by:

- Analyzing work patterns and communication data to predict potential burnout
- Identifying factors that contribute to high team performance
- Suggesting interventions to improve team dynamics and well-being

Case Study: Humu

Humu uses AI to provide personalized recommendations for improving team performance and employee well-being.

Key Features:

1. AI-driven behavioral nudges
2. Predictive analytics for team dynamics
3. Customized recommendations for managers and team members

Results:

- Used by organizations like Walmart and Salesforce
- Improved employee engagement scores by up to 25%
- Reduced turnover rates in high-risk groups by up to 20%

Lesson Learned: AI can help lean startups maintain high team performance while proactively addressing potential burnout and turnover risks.

Potential Challenges and Considerations

While AI offers powerful enhancements to team management and collaboration, it's important to consider potential challenges:

1. **Privacy Concerns**: Collecting and analyzing team data raises important privacy considerations.
2. **Over-reliance on AI**: There's a risk of neglecting human intuition and interpersonal skills in team management.
3. **Integration and Adoption**: Implementing new AI tools may face resistance or require significant change management.
4. **Ethical Considerations**: AI-driven decision-making in team management must be transparent and fair.

Conclusion

The integration of AI into lean team management and collaboration represents a significant advancement in how startups can optimize their most valuable asset: their people. From Forecast's intelligent task allocation to Degreed's skill gap analysis, from Otter.ai's meeting summarization to Humu's performance predictions, we've seen how AI can enhance every aspect of team dynamics.

By leveraging AI, lean startups can make their teams more efficient, adaptive, and resilient. This can lead to faster project completion, more effective skill development, improved communication, and better overall team performance and well-being.

However, it's crucial to remember that AI is a tool to augment human leadership and interpersonal skills, not replace them. The most successful startups will be those that can effectively combine AI-powered insights and automation with empathetic leadership, clear communication, and a strong team culture.

As we move forward, the ability to leverage AI in team management and collaboration will likely become a key competitive advantage for startups. Those who can master this integration will be well-positioned to build high-performing teams, adapt quickly to challenges, and ultimately create more successful and impactful businesses.

Key Takeaways:

1. AI-assisted task allocation and workload balancing can significantly improve team efficiency and project outcomes in lean startup environments.
2. AI-powered skill gap analysis and personalized learning recommendations can help startups build and maintain the right skill sets for success.
3. Automated meeting summarization and action item tracking can save time and improve follow-through in fast-paced startup environments.
4. Predictive analytics for team performance can help startups maintain high productivity while preventing burnout and turnover.
5. While powerful, AI tools in team management come with challenges including privacy concerns, the risk of over-reliance on AI, and the need for careful change management.
6. The most effective approach combines AI-powered tools with empathetic leadership and strong interpersonal skills.
7. Mastering AI-enhanced team management can provide a significant competitive advantage in building and scaling successful startup teams.

"The scale is the hard part. Building the first unit of anything is easy. Building the millionth unit is the hard part."
- Elon Musk

Chapter 14: Scaling with AI: From Startup to Enterprise

Introduction

Throughout our journey exploring the AI-enhanced Lean Startup methodology, we've seen how artificial intelligence can revolutionize various aspects of building and running a startup. From customer discovery to product development, from financial management to team collaboration, AI has demonstrated its transformative potential. Now, we turn our attention to one of the most critical challenges that successful startups face: scaling.

Scaling a startup is a complex process that involves growing your customer base, expanding your operations, and transitioning from a nimble startup to a more structured enterprise. This phase is often make-or-break for many startups, as the strategies and processes that worked in the early stages may not be sufficient for larger-scale operations.

This is where AI can play a crucial role. By leveraging machine learning, predictive analytics, and automation, we can enhance our approach to scaling. From AI-assisted decision making for scaling to automating processes as you grow, from managing AI integration in a growing organization to maintaining the Lean Startup mindset at scale, AI has the potential to make the scaling process more efficient, data-driven, and successful than ever before.

In this chapter, we'll explore how AI is transforming the scaling process for startups, illustrated with real-world case studies. Let's dive into this AI-powered revolution in startup growth and scaling.

1. AI-Assisted Decision Making for Scaling

Making informed decisions about when and how to scale is crucial. AI can assist by:

- Analyzing market trends and internal data to identify optimal scaling opportunities
- Predicting potential challenges and bottlenecks in the scaling process
- Recommending strategies for efficient growth based on successful scaling patterns

Case Study: Crayon

Crayon is an AI-powered competitive intelligence platform that helps companies make data-driven decisions about market expansion and scaling.

Key Features:

1. AI-driven market and competitor analysis
2. Predictive analytics for market opportunities
3. Automated insights for scaling strategies

Results:

- Used by companies like Salesforce, Zendesk, and Adobe
- Helped companies identify new market opportunities, leading to an average revenue increase of 25%
- Reduced time spent on competitive analysis by up to 70%

Lesson Learned: AI-assisted decision making can help startups identify the right moments and strategies for scaling, leading to more successful and efficient growth.

2. Automating Processes as You Grow

As startups scale, automating repetitive tasks becomes crucial for efficiency. AI can help by:

- Identifying processes suitable for automation
- Implementing intelligent automation solutions that can adapt to growing complexity
- Continuously optimizing automated processes based on performance data

Case Study: UiPath

UiPath is a leading Robotic Process Automation (RPA) platform that incorporates AI to help companies automate their processes as they scale.

Key Features:

1. AI-powered process discovery and mapping
2. Intelligent automation with machine learning capabilities
3. Continuous process optimization

Results:

- Used by over 10,000 organizations worldwide
- Helped companies achieve automation rates of up to 80% in certain processes
- Reduced processing times by up to 50% in automated workflows

Lesson Learned: AI-driven process automation can help startups maintain efficiency as they scale, allowing them to handle increased complexity without a proportional increase in resources.

3. Managing AI Integration in a Growing Startup

As startups scale and incorporate more AI solutions, managing these technologies becomes a challenge in itself. Key considerations include:

- Developing an AI governance framework that scales with the company
- Ensuring ethical AI use and maintaining transparency as operations grow
- Building a culture of AI literacy across the expanding organization

Case Study: DataRobot

While primarily an automated machine learning platform, DataRobot also offers solutions for managing AI integration in growing organizations.

Key Features:

1. Centralized AI governance and management
2. Automated documentation for AI model transparency
3. Tools for promoting AI literacy across teams

Results:

- Used by a third of the Fortune 50 companies
- Helped companies reduce model deployment time by up to 90%
- Improved cross-team collaboration on AI projects by up to 60%

Lesson Learned: Proper management of AI integration is crucial for startups as they scale, ensuring that AI remains a valuable asset rather than a source of complexity or risk.

4. Maintaining the Lean Startup Mindset at Scale

As startups grow, maintaining the agility and innovation of the early days can be challenging. AI can help preserve the Lean Startup mindset by:

- Enabling rapid experimentation and A/B testing at scale
- Providing quick, data-driven insights for iterative development
- Facilitating continuous learning and adaptation across the growing organization

Case Study: Optimizely

Optimizely is an experimentation platform that uses AI to help companies maintain a culture of testing and iteration as they scale.

Key Features:

1. AI-powered experiment design and analysis
2. Automated insights generation
3. Personalization at scale

Results:

- Used by companies like IBM, Microsoft, and eBay
- Helped companies run 70% more experiments on average
- Increased conversion rates by up to 30% through continuous optimization

Lesson Learned: AI-enhanced experimentation and learning tools can help startups maintain their innovative edge and Lean Startup principles even as they grow into larger enterprises.

Potential Challenges and Considerations

While AI offers powerful tools for scaling, it's important to consider potential challenges:

1. **Data Quality and Quantity**: As operations scale, ensuring data quality and managing increased data volumes can be challenging.
2. **Ethical Considerations**: Scaling AI use raises important questions about privacy, fairness, and transparency that need to be addressed.
3. **Skill Gap**: Growing startups may struggle to find and retain the AI talent needed to manage and expand their AI initiatives.
4. **Integration Complexity**: As more AI tools are adopted, ensuring they work together seamlessly can become increasingly complex.

Conclusion

The integration of AI into the scaling process represents a significant advancement in how startups can grow into successful enterprises. From Crayon's AI-assisted decision making to UiPath's intelligent process automation, from DataRobot's AI management solutions to Optimizely's experimentation platform, we've seen how AI can enhance every aspect of the scaling journey.

By leveraging AI, startups can make more informed scaling decisions, maintain efficiency as they grow, manage increasing technological complexity, and preserve their innovative culture. This can lead to more successful transitions from startup to enterprise, with less growing pains and more strategic growth.

However, it's crucial to remember that AI is a tool to augment human strategy and decision-making, not replace it. The most successful scaling efforts will be those that effectively combine AI-powered insights and automation with human vision, adaptability, and leadership.

As we move forward, the ability to leverage AI in the scaling process will likely become a key competitive advantage for startups. Those who can master this integration will be well-positioned to grow efficiently, adapt quickly to new challenges, and ultimately build more successful and impactful enterprises.

Key Takeaways:

1. AI-assisted decision making can help startups identify the right moments and strategies for scaling, leading to more successful and efficient growth.
2. AI-driven process automation can help startups maintain efficiency as they scale, handling increased complexity without proportional resource increases.
3. Proper management of AI integration is crucial for startups as they scale, ensuring AI remains a valuable asset rather than a source of complexity or risk.
4. AI-enhanced experimentation and learning tools can help startups maintain their innovative edge and Lean Startup principles even as they grow into larger enterprises.

5. While powerful, AI tools for scaling come with challenges including data management, ethical considerations, skill gaps, and integration complexity.
6. The most effective approach combines AI-powered insights and automation with human vision, adaptability, and leadership.
7. Mastering AI-enhanced scaling strategies can provide a significant competitive advantage in the journey from startup to successful enterprise.

"With great power comes great responsibility."
- Stan Lee

Chapter 15: Ethical Considerations and Challenges in AI-Driven Lean Startups

Introduction

Throughout our exploration of AI-enhanced Lean Startup methodologies, we've witnessed the transformative potential of artificial intelligence across various aspects of building and scaling a startup. From customer discovery to product development, from financial management to scaling strategies, AI has demonstrated its power to revolutionize startup practices. However, with great power comes great responsibility, and the integration of AI into startup operations brings with it a host of ethical considerations and challenges that cannot be ignored.

As lean startups increasingly rely on AI to drive decision-making, automate processes, and interact with customers, they must grapple with questions of data privacy, algorithmic bias, transparency, and the broader societal impacts of their AI-driven innovations. These ethical considerations are not just moral imperatives; they are crucial factors that can significantly impact a startup's reputation, user trust, and long-term success.

In this chapter, we'll delve into the key ethical considerations and challenges that AI-driven lean startups face. We'll explore strategies for addressing these challenges, illustrated with real-world case studies of companies that have navigated these complex issues. By the end of this chapter, you'll have a deeper understanding of how to build not just successful, but also responsible and ethical AI-driven startups.

1. Data Privacy and Security in AI-Driven Startups

As AI systems rely heavily on data, ensuring the privacy and security of user information is paramount. Key considerations include:

- Implementing robust data protection measures
- Ensuring compliance with data privacy regulations (e.g., GDPR, CCPA)
- Balancing data utilization for AI with user privacy rights

Case Study: Privitar

Privitar is a data privacy platform that helps companies, including AI-driven startups, to protect sensitive data while maintaining its utility for AI and analytics.

Key Features:

1. Data anonymization and pseudonymization
2. Privacy-preserving data analytics
3. Centralized privacy policies and controls

Results:

- Used by companies like HSBC, Boots, and NHS Digital
- Helped companies reduce data privacy risks by up to 80%
- Enabled safe use of sensitive data in AI models, increasing available training data by up to 50%

Lesson Learned: Implementing strong data privacy measures is crucial for AI-driven startups to build trust with users and comply with regulations while still leveraging data for innovation.

2. Addressing Bias in AI Systems

AI systems can inadvertently perpetuate or even amplify biases present in their training data or design. Startups must consider:

- Actively identifying and mitigating bias in AI models
- Ensuring diversity in AI development teams
- Regularly auditing AI systems for fairness and equity

Case Study: Fiddler AI

Fiddler AI offers an explainable AI platform that helps companies monitor, explain, and improve their AI models, including detecting and mitigating bias.

Key Features:

1. AI model monitoring and explainability
2. Bias detection and mitigation tools
3. Model performance tracking across different user segments

Results:

- Used by Fortune 500 companies in finance, healthcare, and tech sectors
- Helped companies reduce biased outcomes in AI models by up to 40%

- Improved model transparency, increasing stakeholder trust by up to 60%

Lesson Learned: Actively addressing bias in AI systems is essential for startups to ensure fair and equitable outcomes, maintain user trust, and mitigate regulatory risks.

3. Balancing AI Automation and Human Jobs

As startups increasingly automate processes with AI, they must consider the impact on employment and workforce dynamics. Key considerations include:

- Responsible implementation of AI automation
- Reskilling and upskilling employees for AI-augmented roles
- Maintaining a balance between AI efficiency and human expertise

Case Study: Workday

While not a startup, Workday's approach to AI integration offers valuable lessons. Workday has implemented AI in its HR and financial management software while focusing on augmenting rather than replacing human workers.

Key Features:

1. AI-augmented decision support for HR and finance
2. Machine learning for process optimization
3. Skills-based employee development recommendations

Results:

- Used by thousands of organizations worldwide
- Increased efficiency in HR and finance processes by up to 30%

- Helped companies identify reskilling opportunities, improving internal mobility by up to 20%

Lesson Learned: Startups can leverage AI to improve efficiency while still valuing human expertise and focusing on employee development and augmentation rather than replacement.

4. Ensuring Transparency and Explainability in AI Decision-Making

As AI systems increasingly influence critical decisions, ensuring transparency and explainability becomes crucial. Startups must consider:

- Implementing explainable AI models where possible
- Providing clear information to users about AI's role in decision-making
- Establishing processes for contesting or appealing AI-driven decisions

Case Study: Kyndi

Kyndi is an AI company that focuses on explainable AI, particularly for regulatory and compliance use cases.

Key Features:

1. Natural language processing with explainable results
2. Auditable AI decision-making processes
3. Human-understandable explanations for AI outputs

Results:

- Used by government agencies and Fortune 500 companies
- Improved regulatory compliance rates by up to 35%
- Increased user trust in AI-driven decisions by up to 50%

Lesson Learned: Prioritizing transparency and explainability in AI systems can help startups build trust with users, comply with regulations, and make more responsible use of AI in decision-making processes.

Potential Challenges and Considerations

While addressing these ethical considerations is crucial, startups may face several challenges:

1. **Resource Constraints**: Implementing robust ethical AI practices can be resource-intensive, which may be challenging for early-stage startups.
2. **Rapid Technological Change**: The fast pace of AI development can make it difficult to keep ethical practices up-to-date.
3. **Regulatory Uncertainty**: The evolving landscape of AI regulations can create uncertainty for startups.
4. **Balancing Ethics and Growth**: Startups may face pressure to prioritize rapid growth over ethical considerations.

Conclusion

As we've explored in this chapter, the integration of AI into lean startup methodologies brings not only immense opportunities but also significant ethical challenges. From ensuring data privacy and security to addressing bias in AI systems, from balancing automation with human employment to ensuring transparency in AI decision-making, these ethical considerations are crucial for building responsible and sustainable AI-driven startups.

The case studies we've examined, from Privitar's data privacy solutions to Fiddler AI's bias mitigation tools, from Workday's human-centric AI integration to Kyndi's focus on explainable AI, demonstrate that it is possible to harness the power of AI while still prioritizing ethical considerations.

Moving forward, the most successful AI-driven startups will be those that can effectively balance innovation with responsibility, leveraging AI to drive growth and efficiency while also prioritizing user trust, fairness, and societal impact. By proactively addressing these ethical challenges, startups can not only mitigate risks but also differentiate themselves in the market and build stronger, more sustainable businesses.

As the AI landscape continues to evolve, staying informed about ethical AI practices and actively incorporating them into your startup's DNA will be crucial. Remember, building an ethical AI-driven startup is not just about compliance or risk mitigation – it's about creating technology that truly benefits humanity and contributes positively to society.

Key Takeaways:

1. Ensuring data privacy and security is crucial for AI-driven startups to build trust and comply with regulations while innovating.
2. Actively addressing bias in AI systems is essential for ensuring fair outcomes and maintaining user trust.
3. Balancing AI automation with human expertise and focusing on employee augmentation rather than replacement can lead to more sustainable growth.
4. Prioritizing transparency and explainability in AI systems helps build trust and enables more responsible use of AI in decision-making.
5. While implementing ethical AI practices can be challenging, it's crucial for long-term success and societal impact.
6. Ethical considerations should be integrated into the core of AI-driven startups, not treated as an afterthought.
7. Staying informed about evolving ethical AI practices and regulations is crucial for navigating the rapidly changing AI landscape.

"The best way to predict the future is to invent it."

- Alan Kay

Chapter 16: Future Trends: The Leaner Startup Ecosystem

Introduction

Throughout this book, we've explored how artificial intelligence is revolutionizing the lean startup methodology, from customer discovery to scaling strategies, and even the ethical considerations that arise. As we conclude our journey, it's time to look ahead and consider the future of the AI-driven lean startup ecosystem.

The rapid pace of technological advancement, particularly in AI, promises to further transform how startups are conceived, built, and scaled. In this chapter, we'll explore emerging trends and technologies that are likely to shape the future of lean startups. We'll consider how these developments might change startup practices, create new opportunities, and present new challenges.

From the rise of no-code AI platforms to the potential of quantum computing, from the integration of AI with Internet of Things (IoT) to the emergence of AI-first business models, we'll examine how these trends could make startups even "leaner " and more efficient. Let's dive into this exciting future and consider how entrepreneurs can prepare for the next wave of innovation.

1. No-Code AI and Democratization of AI Development

The trend towards no-code and low-code platforms is extending into AI development, potentially democratizing access to AI capabilities for startups.

Key developments:

- Visual AI model builders requiring little to no coding
- Pre-trained AI models that can be easily customized
- Integration of AI capabilities into popular no-code platforms

Case Study: Obviously AI

Obviously AI is a no-code AI platform that allows users to build and deploy machine learning models without writing code.

Key Features:

1. Drag-and-drop interface for building AI models
2. Automated data preparation and feature engineering
3. One-click deployment of AI models

Potential Impact:

- Could reduce the need for specialized AI talent in early-stage startups
- May accelerate the adoption of AI across various industries

- Might lead to more diverse AI applications as non-technical founders can experiment with AI

Lesson Learned: The democratization of AI development could lower the barrier to entry for AI-driven startups, potentially leading to more innovation and diverse applications of AI in the startup ecosystem.

2. AI-IoT Integration in Lean Hardware Startups

The integration of AI with Internet of Things (IoT) devices is opening new possibilities for lean hardware startups.

Key developments:

- Edge AI enabling smart devices with local processing capabilities
- AI-powered predictive maintenance for IoT devices
- Personalized user experiences through AI-IoT integration

Case Study: Enlighted (acquired by Siemens)

Enlighted develops IoT solutions for smart buildings, integrating AI for energy efficiency and space utilization.

Key Features:

1. AI-powered occupancy detection and space utilization analysis
2. Predictive maintenance for building systems
3. Personalized environmental controls using machine learning

Potential Impact:

- Could enable lean hardware startups to create smarter, more efficient products

- May lead to new business models based on predictive services and personalization
- Might accelerate the development of smart cities and environments

Lesson Learned: The convergence of AI and IoT could create new opportunities for lean hardware startups, enabling them to build more intelligent and efficient physical products.

3. Quantum Computing and Its Impact on AI Startups

While still in early stages, quantum computing has the potential to significantly enhance AI capabilities, opening new frontiers for startups.

Key developments:

- Quantum machine learning algorithms
- Quantum-enhanced optimization for complex AI models
- Potential breakthroughs in natural language processing and computer vision

Case Study: Zapata Computing

Zapata Computing is a startup focused on quantum-enabled AI solutions.

Key Features:

1. Quantum machine learning platforms
2. Hybrid quantum-classical algorithms for near-term quantum computers
3. Quantum-inspired AI optimization techniques

Potential Impact:

- Could enable AI to tackle currently unsolvable problems

- May lead to breakthroughs in drug discovery, financial modeling, and cryptography
- Might create a new category of quantum-AI startups

Lesson Learned: While still emerging, quantum computing could dramatically enhance AI capabilities, potentially creating new categories of AI applications and startups.

4. AI-First Business Models

As AI capabilities advance, we may see the emergence of entirely new business models that are fundamentally enabled by AI.

Key developments:

- Hyper-personalized services powered by AI
- AI-as-a-Service platforms for specific industries
- Autonomous AI agents capable of complex decision-making

Case Study: Lemonade Insurance

While not a new startup, Lemonade's AI-first approach to insurance offers insights into future AI-driven business models.

Key Features:

1. AI-powered underwriting and claims processing
2. Behavioral economics and machine learning for fraud detection
3. Chatbots for customer service and policy management

Potential Impact:

- Could lead to more efficient, personalized services across various industries
- May enable new forms of value creation and capture

- Might challenge traditional business models in many sectors

Lesson Learned: AI-first business models could redefine entire industries, creating opportunities for startups to disrupt established markets with highly efficient and personalized services.

Potential Challenges and Considerations

As we look to this AI-driven future, several challenges and considerations emerge:

1. **Ethical and Regulatory Landscape**: As AI becomes more pervasive, navigating evolving ethical guidelines and regulations will be crucial.
2. **AI Talent Shortage**: Despite no-code solutions, the demand for specialized AI talent may continue to outstrip supply.
3. **Data Quality and Availability**: As AI models become more sophisticated, ensuring access to high-quality, diverse datasets will be increasingly important.
4. **Explainability and Trust**: As AI systems make more critical decisions, ensuring their explainability and building public trust will be essential.

Conclusion

The future of the lean startup ecosystem is inextricably linked with the advancement of AI technologies. From the democratization of AI development through no-code platforms to the potential quantum leap in AI capabilities through quantum computing, from the convergence of AI and IoT to the emergence of AI-first business models, these trends promise to make startups even "leaner ," more efficient, and more innovative.

These developments have the potential to lower barriers to entry, accelerate the pace of innovation, and open up entirely new markets and business models. However, they also bring challenges, from ethical considerations to talent shortages, that startups will need to navigate carefully.

As we stand on the brink of this AI-driven future, it's clear that the most successful startups will be those that can not only leverage these emerging technologies but also adapt quickly to the changing landscape. They will need to balance the pursuit of AI-driven efficiency and innovation with ethical considerations and human-centric values.

For entrepreneurs and startup founders, staying informed about these trends and actively exploring how they can be applied to solve real-world problems will be crucial. The future belongs to those who can harness the power of AI to create value in new and unexpected ways, while building responsible and sustainable businesses.

Key Takeaways:

1. No-code AI platforms could democratize AI development, lowering barriers to entry for AI-driven startups.
2. The integration of AI and IoT presents new opportunities for lean hardware startups to create smarter, more efficient products.
3. Quantum computing, while still emerging, has the potential to dramatically enhance AI capabilities and create new categories of startups.
4. AI-first business models could redefine entire industries, creating opportunities for highly efficient and personalized services.
5. Navigating ethical considerations, talent shortages, and data quality issues will be crucial challenges in this AI-driven future.
6. Successful startups will need to balance AI-driven innovation with responsible and ethical business practices.

7. Staying informed and adaptable will be key for entrepreneurs looking to thrive in the evolving AI-driven lean startup ecosystem.

"The future belongs to those who believe in the beauty of their dreams."
- Eleanor Roosevelt

Chapter 17: Building the Future with Leaner Startups and GenAI

Introduction

As we reach the conclusion of our exploration into the synergy between Lean Startup methodologies and Generative AI (GenAI), it's time to reflect on the transformative journey we've undertaken. Throughout this book, we've delved into how AI is revolutionizing every aspect of the startup lifecycle, from ideation to scaling, and even the ethical considerations that arise along the way.

In this final chapter, we'll summarize the key insights from our journey, reflect on the implications for entrepreneurs and the startup ecosystem, and look ahead to the exciting future that awaits at the intersection of Lean Startup principles and advanced AI technologies.

Key Insights Recap

Let's revisit some of the crucial insights we've gained throughout this book:

1. **The Evolution of Lean Startup with GenAI**: We began by tracing the evolution from traditional Lean Startup methods to the AI-enhanced approaches of today. GenAI has amplified the core principles of rapid iteration, customer-centricity, and data-driven decision making.
2. **AI-Enhanced Business Model Generation**: We explored how AI can supercharge the process of creating and refining business models, from automated market research to AI-powered value proposition design.
3. **Rapid Prototyping and MVP Development**: We saw how GenAI is revolutionizing the creation of Minimum Viable Products, enabling startups to test ideas faster and more efficiently than ever before.
4. **Optimizing the Build-Measure-Learn Cycle**: AI's role in accelerating and enhancing each phase of this crucial cycle was examined, showing how startups can iterate and improve at unprecedented speeds.
5. **AI-Powered Customer Discovery and Validation**: We delved into how AI is transforming the way startups understand and validate their customers, from automated interview analysis to AI-generated customer personas.
6. **Growth Hacking and Marketing with AI**: The power of AI in supercharging growth strategies was explored, from content generation to predictive analytics for customer acquisition.
7. **Lean Analytics in the AI Era**: We examined how AI is reshaping the way startups measure and analyze their progress, enabling more accurate and actionable insights.
8. **AI in Team Management and Collaboration**: The role of AI in enhancing team dynamics and productivity in lean startups was discussed, highlighting both opportunities and challenges.

9. **Scaling with AI**: We explored how AI can assist startups in navigating the complex process of scaling, from decision support to process automation.
10. **Ethical Considerations in AI-Driven Startups**: The crucial ethical challenges that arise with increased AI adoption were examined, emphasizing the importance of responsible AI use.
11. **Future Trends in AI and Lean Startups**: Finally, we looked ahead to emerging trends that promise to further transform the startup landscape, from no-code AI to quantum computing.

Implications for Entrepreneurs and the Startup Ecosystem

The integration of GenAI into Lean Startup methodologies has profound implications:

1. **Democratization of Innovation**: With AI lowering barriers to entry, we can expect to see a more diverse range of entrepreneurs and ideas entering the startup ecosystem.
2. **Accelerated Pace of Innovation**: AI-driven efficiencies will likely lead to faster iteration cycles and quicker time-to-market for new products and services.
3. **Shift in Required Skill Sets**: While AI will automate many tasks, it will also create demand for new skills at the intersection of business, technology, and ethics.
4. **New Business Models**: AI-first startups will emerge, creating entirely new categories of products and services that were previously unimaginable.
5. **Ethical Innovation**: Successful startups of the future will need to prioritize ethical considerations alongside growth and profitability.

The Road Ahead: Building Leaner Startups with GenAI

As we look to the future, several key principles will guide the development of truly Leaner Startups powered by GenAI:

1. **Continuous AI Integration**: Startups must view AI not as a one-time implementation, but as a core component that evolves with the business.
2. **Human-AI Collaboration**: The most successful startups will be those that effectively balance AI capabilities with human creativity and intuition.
3. **Ethical AI by Design**: Building ethical considerations into AI systems from the ground up will be crucial for long-term success and societal benefit.
4. **Adaptive Learning**: In a rapidly evolving tech landscape, startups must cultivate a culture of continuous learning and adaptation.
5. **Global Perspective**: As AI enables easier global reach, startups must think globally from day one, considering diverse markets and cultural contexts.

Conclusion

The convergence of Lean Startup methodologies and Generative AI marks a new era in entrepreneurship. It offers unprecedented opportunities for innovation, efficiency, and impact. However, it also brings new challenges and responsibilities.

As we stand at this exciting juncture, it's clear that the startups that will thrive are those that can harness the power of AI to amplify the core principles of the Lean Startup approach: rapid iteration, customer-centricity, and data-driven decision making. At the same time, they must navigate the ethical implications of AI and contribute positively to society.

The future of startups is leaner, smarter, and more impactful than ever before. It's a future where AI augments human creativity, where data-driven decisions are made in real-time, and where innovations can scale rapidly to address global challenges.

To the entrepreneurs embarking on this journey: embrace the power of GenAI, stay true to Lean Startup principles, and never lose sight of the human element in your quest to change the world. The future is yours to build.

Key Takeaways:

1. GenAI has transformed every aspect of the Lean Startup methodology, from ideation to scaling.
2. AI-driven efficiencies are accelerating innovation cycles and democratizing entrepreneurship.
3. New skills at the intersection of business, technology, and ethics are becoming crucial for startup success.
4. Ethical considerations must be at the forefront of AI implementation in startups.
5. Successful startups of the future will balance AI capabilities with human creativity and intuition.
6. Continuous learning and adaptation are essential in the rapidly evolving AI landscape.
7. The future of startups is leaner, smarter, and poised to create unprecedented global impact.

Practical Guide: Using GPT-4 for Market Research and Customer Segmentation

Introduction

In this section, we'll explore how to leverage GPT-4, a powerful generative AI model, for market research and customer segmentation. While GPT-4 isn't specifically designed for these tasks, its advanced language understanding and generation capabilities make it a versatile tool that can assist in various aspects of market analysis.

Getting Started with GPT-4

To use GPT-4, you'll need access to a platform that offers the model, such as OpenAI's API or ChatGPT. For this guide, we'll assume you're using ChatGPT with GPT-4.

1. Market Research

Step 1: Define Your Research Objectives

Start by clearly defining what you want to know. For example: "I want to understand the current trends in the sustainable fashion market."

Step 2: Ask GPT-4 for an Overview

Prompt: "Provide an overview of the current trends in the sustainable fashion market."

GPT-4 will generate a summary of trends based on its training data. Remember, its knowledge has a cutoff date, so always cross-reference with current sources.

Step 3: Dive Deeper into Specific Areas

Based on the overview, ask more specific questions. For example: "What are the main challenges facing sustainable fashion brands?" "Who are the leading companies in sustainable fashion, and what sets them apart?"

Step 4: Analyze Competitors

Prompt: "Analyze the strengths and weaknesses of the top 3 sustainable fashion brands."

Step 5: Identify Potential Opportunities

Prompt: "Based on the current trends and challenges in sustainable fashion, what potential opportunities exist for new entrants in the market?"

2. Customer Segmentation

Step 1: Define Your Target Market

Prompt: "Help me define potential customer segments for a sustainable fashion brand targeting millennials."

Step 2: Create Detailed Personas

For each identified segment, create a detailed persona. Prompt: "Create a detailed persona for an eco-conscious millennial fashion consumer. Include demographics, psychographics, behaviors, and preferences."

Step 3: Identify Key Characteristics

Prompt: "What are the top 5 characteristics that differentiate various customer segments in the sustainable fashion market?"

Step 4: Understand Segment Needs

For each segment, delve into their specific needs and pain points. Prompt: "What are the main pain points and needs of the eco-conscious millennial fashion consumer segment?"

Step 5: Segment Validation Ideas

Prompt: "Suggest methods to validate these customer segments and gather real-world data to refine our understanding."

Best Practices and Limitations

1. **Use GPT-4 as a Starting Point**: The information provided should be a springboard for further research, not the end point.
2. **Verify Information**: Always cross-check important information with reliable, up-to-date sources.
3. **Refine Your Prompts**: The quality of output depends on the quality of your prompts. Be specific and iterative in your questioning.
4. **Combine with Other Tools**: Use GPT-4 in conjunction with traditional market research tools and methodologies for comprehensive insights.
5. **Be Aware of Biases**: GPT-4 may reflect biases present in its training data. Be critical and aware of potential biases in the generated content.
6. **Respect Privacy and Ethics**: Do not use GPT-4 to generate or process personal data or sensitive information.

Important Considerations

While GPT-4 can be a powerful tool for market research and customer segmentation, it's crucial to be aware of its limitations and potential pitfalls:

1. **Potential for "Hallucinations"**: GPT-4, like other large language models, can occasionally produce convincing but incorrect information. This phenomenon is often referred to as "hallucination." Always fact-check important information generated by GPT-4, especially when it relates to specific facts, figures, or recent events.
2. **Lack of Comprehensive Studies**: The effectiveness of using GPT-4 for market research and customer segmentation tasks has not been comprehensively studied or compared to traditional methods. Results may vary depending on the specific use case, prompt quality, and other factors. It's advisable to use GPT-4 in conjunction with established research methods rather than as a replacement.
3. **No Real-Time Data or Primary Research Capabilities**: While GPT-4 can provide insights based on its training data, it doesn't have access to real-time information or the ability to conduct primary research. Its knowledge is limited to its training cutoff date. For comprehensive market analysis, it's crucial to complement GPT-4's insights with up-to-date data and primary research methods such as surveys, interviews, and direct observation.
4. **Potential Biases**: Like any AI model, GPT-4 may reflect biases present in its training data. Be aware of this when interpreting its outputs, especially when dealing with sensitive topics or diverse markets.
5. **Lack of Domain-Specific Expertise**: While GPT-4 has broad knowledge, it may lack the nuanced understanding that industry experts possess. Its insights should be validated by professionals with relevant experience in your specific market.
6. **Consistency Issues**: GPT-4 may provide different responses to the same query asked multiple times. This

inconsistency means that a single response shouldn't be taken as definitive without further verification.

By keeping these considerations in mind, you can more effectively leverage GPT-4 as part of your market research and customer segmentation toolkit, while avoiding potential pitfalls and ensuring a more robust analysis.

Conclusion

GPT-4 can be a powerful tool for initial market research and customer segmentation, providing quick insights and ideas. However, it should be used as part of a broader research strategy that includes traditional methods, primary research, and expert analysis. By combining the speed and breadth of AI-generated insights with human expertise and real-world data, startups can develop a more comprehensive and accurate understanding of their market and customers.

By understanding both the potential and the limitations of GPT-4, startups can leverage this powerful tool effectively while maintaining the rigor and comprehensiveness required for sound market research and customer segmentation.

General Learnings: What to Be Cautious of as a Startup Founder

Drawing from over 25 years of experience as a founder since the Dotcom era, here are some key learnings on things to be cautious about as a startup founder. These are not meant to be entirely avoided, but rather to be approached with careful consideration and prioritization. Remember, while these activities can be beneficial, they can also distract from the core objective of building a successful startup.

1. Startup Meetups & Conferences vs. Industry-Specific Events

Caution: Spending too much time at general startup events instead of industry-specific conferences.

Why it's tempting: Startup events are exciting, full of energy, and can provide networking opportunities with other entrepreneurs and investors.

The risk: You may find yourself in an echo chamber, disconnected from the real problems and opportunities in your target industry.

Better approach: Prioritize attending conferences and meetups specific to the industry you're trying to disrupt. This is where you'll meet potential customers, partners, and gain invaluable industry insights.

2. Following Startup Ecosystems vs. Deep Industry Knowledge

Caution: Obsessing over other startups and ecosystem news instead of deepening your understanding of your target industry.

Why it's tempting: Startup news is often exciting and can feel relevant to your journey.

The risk: You may lose focus on your specific market and miss crucial industry trends or opportunities.

Better approach: While staying informed about the startup world is important, invest more time in becoming an expert in the industry you're disrupting. Read industry publications, follow key thought leaders, and engage with potential customers.

3. Chasing Funding Metrics Over Revenue Metrics

Caution: Focusing more on metrics that appeal to investors rather than those that indicate real business health and customer value.

Why it's tempting: Funding rounds make headlines and can validate your idea in the short term.

The risk: You may build a company that's good at raising money but struggles to create sustainable value for customers.

Better approach: Prioritize metrics that reflect customer satisfaction, product-market fit, and revenue growth. These will not only build a sustainable business but will also make you more attractive to investors in the long run.

4. Perfecting the Product vs. Getting Market Feedback

Caution: Spending too much time perfecting your product before getting it in front of real users.

Why it's tempting: It's natural to want your product to be "perfect" before launching.

The risk: You may spend resources building features that users don't actually want or need.

Better approach: Embrace the MVP (Minimum Viable Product) approach. Launch earlier with core features and iterate based on real user feedback.

5. Building a Large Team vs. Staying Lean

Caution: Rapidly expanding your team before you've achieved product-market fit.

Why it's tempting: A larger team can feel like progress and can be attractive to investors.

The risk: Increased burn rate and complexity before you've validated your business model.

Better approach: Stay lean until you've proven product-market fit. Use contractors or part-time help to fill gaps in expertise when needed.

6. Chasing Press Coverage vs. Building Customer Relationships

Caution: Prioritizing media attention over building strong customer relationships.

Why it's tempting: Press coverage can feel validating and potentially attract investors or partners.

The risk: You may focus on crafting a compelling story for the media rather than solving real customer problems.

Better approach: Focus on delighting your customers. Happy customers can become your best marketers and can provide testimonials that are more valuable than press coverage.

7. Copying Competitors vs. Innovating

Caution: Spending too much time and energy reacting to competitors' moves instead of charting your own course.

Why it's tempting: It can feel safer to follow a path that others have already validated.

The risk: You may always be one step behind, rather than creating unique value for your customers.

Better approach: While it's important to be aware of your competitive landscape, focus more on your unique vision and the specific problems you're solving for your customers.

8. Targeting Broad Markets vs. Narrow Segmentation

Caution: Aiming for a broad, large market instead of focusing on a narrow, well-defined customer segment.

Why it's tempting: A larger market seems to offer more opportunities and can be more attractive to investors. It feels like you're limiting your potential by narrowing your focus.

The risk: You may spread your resources too thin, fail to differentiate from incumbents, and struggle to establish a strong market position. Your message and product may resonate with no one by trying to appeal to everyone.

Better approach: Focus on a narrow, well-defined market segment. This counterintuitive strategy often leads to higher chances of success for several reasons:

1. **Clear differentiation**: A narrow focus allows you to tailor your product precisely to the needs of a specific group, setting you apart from broader, less-specialized solutions.
2. **Word-of-mouth growth**: When you solve specific problems for a well-defined group, word spreads quickly within that community.
3. **Efficient resource use**: Limited resources can be used more effectively when targeting a specific segment.
4. **Easier positioning against incumbents**: Large competitors often can't or won't cater to very specific needs, giving you a clear angle for differentiation.
5. **Deeper understanding**: A narrow focus allows you to become a true expert in your customers' needs, leading to better products and stronger relationships.
6. **Easier marketing and sales**: Your message can be much more targeted and effective when speaking to a well-defined audience.

Remember, many successful companies started with a narrow focus and expanded later. Facebook started with college students, Amazon with books, and Uber with high-end rides in San Francisco.

By deeply understanding and serving a specific segment, you build a strong foundation from which you can expand. It's often easier to expand from a strong position in a small market than to try to capture a small piece of a large market.

Conclusion

While none of these activities are inherently bad, and each can have its place in your startup journey, the key is prioritization. Always ask yourself: "Is this activity directly contributing to solving our customers' problems and growing our business?" If not, it might be a distraction.

From avoiding the allure of broad markets to prioritizing industry-specific knowledge, these learnings highlight the importance of focus and strategic prioritization in the startup journey. By keeping these cautions in mind, including the counterintuitive value of narrow market segmentation, founders can navigate the complex startup landscape more effectively, increasing their chances of building a successful and impactful company.

Bibliography

Agrawal, A., Gans, J., & Goldfarb, A. (2018). Prediction Machines: The Simple Economics of Artificial Intelligence. Harvard Business Review Press.

Blank, S. (2013). The Four Steps to the Epiphany: Successful Strategies for Products that Win. K&S Ranch.

Brynjolfsson, E., & McAfee, A. (2017). Machine, Platform, Crowd: Harnessing Our Digital Future. W. W. Norton & Company.

Croll, A., & Yoskovitz, B. (2013). Lean Analytics: Use Data to Build a Better Startup Faster. O'Reilly Media.

Domingos, P. (2015). The Master Algorithm: How the Quest for the Ultimate Learning Machine Will Remake Our World. Basic Books.

Ertel, W. (2017). Introduction to Artificial Intelligence. Springer.

Fried, J., & Hansson, D. H. (2010). Rework. Crown Business.

Gero, J. S., & Hanna, S. (2015). Design Computing and Cognition '14. Springer.

Goodfellow, I., Bengio, Y., & Courville, A. (2016). Deep Learning. MIT Press.

Hofmann, M., & Klinkenberg, R. (2013). RapidMiner: Data Mining Use Cases and Business Analytics Applications. Chapman and Hall/CRC.

Humble, J., Molesky, J., & O'Reilly, B. (2015). Lean Enterprise: How High Performance Organizations Innovate at Scale. O'Reilly Media.

Kelleher, J. D., & Tierney, B. (2018). Data Science. MIT Press.

Kotler, P., & Armstrong, G. (2017). Principles of Marketing. Pearson.

Lee, K. F. (2018). AI Superpowers: China, Silicon Valley, and the New World Order. Houghton Mifflin Harcourt.

Maurya, A. (2012). Running Lean: Iterate from Plan A to a Plan That Works. O'Reilly Media.

Ng, A. (2020). Machine Learning Yearning: Technical Strategy for AI Engineers, In the Era of Deep Learning. deeplearning.ai.

O'Neil, C. (2016). Weapons of Math Destruction: How Big Data Increases Inequality and Threatens Democracy. Crown.

Osterwalder, A., & Pigneur, Y. (2010). Business Model Generation: A Handbook for Visionaries, Game Changers, and Challengers. John Wiley & Sons.

Ries, E. (2011). The Lean Startup: How Today's Entrepreneurs Use Continuous Innovation to Create Radically Successful Businesses. Crown Business.

Russell, S., & Norvig, P. (2020). Artificial Intelligence: A Modern Approach (4th Edition). Pearson.

Segaran, T. (2007). Programming Collective Intelligence: Building Smart Web 2.0 Applications. O'Reilly Media.

Sutton, R. S., & Barto, A. G. (2018). Reinforcement Learning: An Introduction. MIT Press.

Thiel, P., & Masters, B. (2014). Zero to One: Notes on Startups, or How to Build the Future. Crown Business.

Topol, E. J. (2019). Deep Medicine: How Artificial Intelligence Can Make Healthcare Human Again. Basic Books.

Varian, H. R., & Farrell, J. (2004). The Economics of Information Technology: An Introduction. Cambridge University Press.

Glossary

A/B Testing: A method of comparing two versions of a product or marketing material to determine which performs better.

Agile: A project management and product development approach that emphasizes flexibility, customer feedback, and rapid iterations.

Algorithm: A set of rules or instructions given to an AI, neural network, or other machine to help it learn on its own.

Artificial Intelligence (AI): The simulation of human intelligence processes by machines, especially computer systems.

Bias (in AI): Systematic errors in AI systems that can lead to unfair outcomes, often reflecting societal or data biases.

Big Data: Extremely large data sets that may be analyzed computationally to reveal patterns, trends, and associations.

Build-Measure-Learn: The core component of the Lean Startup methodology, emphasizing rapid iteration and learning.

Burn Rate: The rate at which a company is losing money, typically expressed as a monthly rate.

Business Model Canvas: A strategic management template for developing new or documenting existing business models.

Chat GPT: A large language model developed by OpenAI, capable of generating human-like text based on input prompts.

Customer Development: A framework for discovering and validating the right market for your idea, developed by Steve Blank.

Data Mining: The process of discovering patterns in large data sets involving methods at the intersection of machine learning, statistics, and database systems.

Deep Learning: A subset of machine learning based on artificial neural networks with multiple layers.

Disruptive Innovation: An innovation that creates a new market and value network, eventually disrupting existing markets and firms.

Ethereum: An open-source, blockchain-based platform that enables smart contracts and decentralized applications (dApps).

Generative AI (GenAI): AI systems that can create new content, including text, images, audio, and synthetic data.

Growth Hacking: A marketing technique focused on rapid experimentation across marketing channels and product development to identify the most efficient ways to grow a business.

Internet of Things (IoT): The interconnection via the internet of computing devices embedded in everyday objects, enabling them to send and receive data.

Lean Analytics: The use of data to measure progress, identify problems, and make decisions in a lean startup context.

Lean Canvas: A 1-page business plan template adapted from the Business Model Canvas, designed for lean startups.

Machine Learning: A subset of AI that provides systems the ability to automatically learn and improve from experience without being explicitly programmed.

Minimum Viable Product (MVP): A product with enough features to attract early-adopter customers and validate a product idea early in the development cycle.

Natural Language Processing (NLP): A branch of AI that deals with the interaction between computers and humans using natural language.

Neural Network: A series of algorithms that attempt to recognize underlying relationships in a set of data through a process that mimics the way the human brain operates.

Pivot: A structured course correction designed to test a new fundamental hypothesis about the product, strategy, and engine of growth.

Product-Market Fit: The degree to which a product satisfies a strong market demand.

Quantum Computing: A type of computation that harnesses the collective properties of quantum states, such as superposition, interference, and entanglement, to perform calculations.

Reinforcement Learning: An area of machine learning concerned with how software agents ought to take actions in an environment to maximize some notion of cumulative reward.

Runway: The amount of time until a company runs out of cash, assuming current income and expenses stay constant.

Scalability: The capability of a system, network, or process to handle a growing amount of work, or its potential to be enlarged to accommodate that growth.

Startup: A company or project undertaken by an entrepreneur to seek, develop, and validate a scalable business model.

Supervised Learning: A type of machine learning where the algorithm learns on a labeled dataset, providing an answer key that the algorithm can use to evaluate its accuracy on training data.

Unsupervised Learning: A type of machine learning where the algorithm learns from unlabeled data, trying to find hidden structures in the data.

Validation: The process of testing and proving (or disproving) assumptions about your business idea in a scientific and methodical way.

Venture Capital: A form of private equity financing that is provided by venture capital firms or funds to startups, early-stage, and emerging companies that have been deemed to have high growth potential.

About the Author

Arup Maity is a seasoned tech entrepreneur and thought leader at the forefront of AI-driven innovation in both software development and construction management. With over two decades of experience as the President and CEO of BlastAsia, a leading software product engineering company,

Arup has consistently pushed the boundaries of digital transformation. His current ventures, Steer and Xamun, exemplify his commitment to leveraging AI for practical business solutions - Steer revolutionizing project monitoring in construction, while Xamun makes ground up software development easier and faster than every before.

As an adjunct faculty member at the Asian Institute of Management and a director of the Philippine Software Industry Association, Arup brings a unique blend of academic insight and industry expertise to his writing. His multifaceted background, spanning from civil engineering to MBA-level business acumen, provides him with a holistic perspective on the intersection of AI, digital strategy, and real-world application. In this book, Arup distills his vast experience and forward-thinking approach to offer readers a comprehensive guide to navigating the AI-driven future of business and technology.

www.ingramcontent.com/pod-product-compliance
Lightning Source LLC
Chambersburg PA
CBHW052209220526
45471CB00004B/1890